Books by Harvey Frommer

The Martial Arts: Judo and Karate
A Sailing Primer (WITH RON WEINMANN)
A Baseball Century

The Martial Arts:
Judo and Karate

The Martial Arts:

NEW YORK   1978   ATHENEUM

Judo and Karate

HARVEY FROMMER

796.8152
F932

Library of Congress Cataloging in Publication Data

Frommer, Harvey.
   The martial arts—judo and karate.
   1. Judo. 2. Karate. I. Title.
GV1114.F76 1978   796.8'152   78-55205
ISBN 0-689-10908-3

Copyright © 1978 by Harvey Frommer
All rights reserved
Published simultaneously in Canada by McClelland and Stewart, Ltd.
Composition by Connecticut Printers, Inc., Hartford, Connecticut
Printed and bound by Halliday Lithograph Corp., Hanover, Massachusetts
Designed by Kathleen Carey
First Edition

To my gentle children:
JENNIFER, FREDDY, IAN.

Acknowledgments

This book would not have been possible without the able assistance of a number of people. To Marvin Brown, thanks for direction and encouragement. To Paul Russell Rogg, owner-instructor at the RPR School of Self-Defense, Whitestone, New York, and Hank Levine, my appreciation for patient posing. Thanks also to Lina Rivera for photographic assistance in the Judo portion of the book.

A special thanks to Steve Gross for advice, direction, posing and most competent assistance.

With this book, as with all my projects, my deepest debt is owed to my wife, Myrna—for typing, editing, organizing, criticizing and inspiring.

Harvey Frommer
1978

Neither the author nor the publishers assumes or accepts any responsibility or liability for any possible injuries sustained by anyone as the result of the use or practice of any instructions contained in this book.

Contents

JUDO: THE "GENTLE" SPORT   7

A BRIEF HISTORY   7
THE NATURE OF THE SPORT   8
THE FORMALITY AND ETIQUETTE OF JUDO   9
JUDO RANKS   11
JUDO AND YOUR BODY   12
BREAKFALLS *(Ukemi)*   18
THROWING TECHNIQUES *(Nage Waza)*   22
TYPES OF THROWS   24
    Foot and Leg Techniques *(Ashi Waza)*   25
    Hip Techniques *(Koshi Waza)*   38
    Hand Techniques *(Te Waza)*   44
    Sacrifice Techniques *(Utemi Waza)*   47
    Hold-Downs *(Osae Komi Waza)*   51
    Choking Techniques *(Shime Waza)*   57
    Armlock Techniques *(Kansetsu Waza)*   62

KARATE: THE "POWER" SPORT   65

A BRIEF HISTORY   65
THE NATURE OF THE SPORT   67
THE KARATE SHOUT—THE KEE-UP *(Kiai)*   68
THE UNIFORM AND THE BOW   70
THE STANCE *(Dachi)*   70
THE KARATE FIST   79
PUNCHING *(Zuki)*   81

CONTENTS

STRIKING *(Uchi)*	87
BLOCKING *(Uke)*	92
KICKING *(Geri)*	100
SPARRING *(Kumite)*	108
THE ENERGY OF KARATE	109
PSYCHOLOGICAL ENERGY OF KARATE	112

TIPS FROM THE PROS — 114

GLOSSARY — 119
    JUDO — 119
    KARATE — 121

APPENDIX A — 123
    Summary Sketches of Four Other Eastern Martial Arts — 123

APPENDIX B — 125
    Judo Contest Calls — 125

The Martial Arts:
Judo and Karate

Introduction

DESPITE THE MAGIC of trick photography and stunt men in movies and television programs, the martial arts are not miracle workers. *Judo, karate, kung fu, aikido, kendo* . . . the names are exotic, but all these sports are useless if you approach them with an exotic attitude. They require discipline, concentration, willingness to learn, and proper mental attitude. The martial arts train the body, but they also—as you will learn firsthand—do wonders for the mind and the spirit.

This book presents an overview of the basics of judo and karate. It is by no means the last word, but it is a starting point. As one interested in the Eastern martial arts, you will join not only millions of people all over the world, but also such celebrities as Ryan O'Neal, Steve McQueen, James Caan, Peter Fonda, Herb Alpert, James

INTRODUCTION

Coburn, Robert Goulet, Mike Connors. Whether a celebrity or an ordinary person, attitude is most important.

Do not be concerned about showing off your stance. Do not be overly concerned about the way your uniform looks to others. Do not brag about the way you are progressing. Do not ever use the skills you are acquiring to hurt or to bully another person.

A trio of quotations from figures identified with the martial arts should give you further insights into the mystique and the practical aspects of these sports.

The legendary Bruce Lee said, "The matter of breaking bricks and boards with the edge of your hand . . . how often do you ever see a brick or a board pick a fight with anybody? This is gimmick stuff. A human being just doesn't stand there and wait to be hit."

David Carradine, star of the television show "Kung Fu," said, "I was only a dancer and an actor. I did the fight scenes for the show by having each move carefully rehearsed."

Professor Jigoro Kano, founder of the Kodokan judo, said:

> What then does this "gentleness" or giving way "really mean?" To answer this question, let us suppose that we estimate the strength of a man in units of one. Let us say that the strength of a man standing in front of me is represented by 10 units whereas my strength, less than his, is represented by 7 units. Now if he pushes me with all his force, I

shall certainly be pushed back or thrown down, even if I used all my strength against his . . . because I used all my strength against him opposing strength with strength. But if, instead of opposing him, I were to give way to his strength by withdrawing my body just as much as he had pushed, taking care at the same time to keep my balance, then he would naturally lean forward and thus lose his balance.

In this new position, he may have become so weak (not in actual physical strength but because of his awkward position) as to have his strength represented for the moment by only three units, instead of his normal 10 units. But meanwhile, by keeping my balance, I retain my full strength as originally represented by 7 units. Here only half my strength is used, that is, half of my seven units, or three and one half against his three. This leaves one half of my strength available for any purpose. Now, if I had greater strength than my opponent, I could of course push him back. But even if I wished to push him back and had the power to do so, it would still be better for me first to give way, because by so doing I should have greatly economized my energy and exhausted my opponent's.

Both judo and karate have the practical advantage of allowing each individual to participate within his or her physical limitations. You can work on skill development

INTRODUCTION

in a small area. Hardly any equipment is needed. You can make good progress in a fairly short time period. You can study alone or with a partner, or join a school and work under the supervision of a teacher. If you go the route of getting a teacher and a school—and this is recommended—act with care. Ask for references. Seek advice from physical education teachers or write to martial arts magazines.

Exercises before or after your judo or karate moves will be of great help in your development. Just as basketball and baseball players and other athletes warm up, you should warm up and also unwind. Neck twisting—up-and-down, side-to-side, and in a circular motion—is one good calisthenic. Rotation of your body, especially your knees, is another. Sit-ups, push-ups and knee-bends are all good conditioners.

Judo and karate should be approached with caution and care. At first, perform some of the more challenging maneuvers in slow motion. If you work with a friend or partner, don't compete—cooperate.

Finally, read and reread the pages of this book. Study the photographs. Learn the vocabulary in the glossary. What you actually have is two books in one. Get set to apply yourself and to experience an adventure—a triple adventure of body, mind, spirit.

JUDO:
The "Gentle" Sport

A BRIEF HISTORY

JI-JITSU CAME into being in Japan thousands of years ago. At first, only Samurai warriors were permitted to study the sport. By the 1850's, different ji-jitsu schools existed all over Japan. Each one went its own way and seemed to have its own secrets, its own approaches.

Professor Jigoro Kano, a man frustrated by the different approaches and by what he saw as the violence of some of the schools, founded what we know today as judo. Kano did this in 1882, calling the new sport *judo*, which means "the gentle way." Out went the dangerous moves, such as foot and hand strikes, and in came some of the old ji-jitsu methods together with some new techniques. One of the basic but very important approaches

Professor Kano taught was that it was wrong to hurt or even compete against another person in judo if that opponent was less skillful than you.

Many trace judo's beginnings in the United States to President Theodore Roosevelt, a believer in a keen mind and a strong body. After Roosevelt witnessed a judo contest, he was so impressed that he imported his own Japanese judo instructor. After World War II, judo really began to catch on as a sport in the United States. In 1953, the American Amateur Athletic Union recognized judo as a sport. By 1964, judo was an official Olympic sport. Today thousands and thousands of people of all ages participate in this sport.

THE NATURE OF THE SPORT

Judo teaches you how to defend yourself by using speed, agility and timing against an opponent through control of your body and efficient use of the least amount of strength. The basic focus of the sport is to give way to strength, to resist an attack, to counter an attack. It is almost impossible to use judo effectively unless you are being attacked.

Judo's founder, Professor Kano, had this to say about the meaning and nature of the sport:

> . . . judo is the means of understanding the way to make the most effective use of both physical and

spiritual power and strength. By devoted practice and rigid discipline in an effort to attain perfection in attacking and defending, it refines the body and soul and helps instill the spiritual essence of judo into every part of one's being. In this way it is possible to perfect oneself and contribute something worthwhile to the world.

A final point about the nature of the sport: Size is really not that important. Sometimes, the bigger they are, the harder they fall. You will probably delight in learning this final point firsthand as you put the principles of judo into practice.

THE FORMALITY AND ETIQUETTE OF JUDO

Judo is not street-fighting. As Dr. Kano observed, it is a sport that has certain inner values. Important rules, regulations, customs exist for the safety and the development of judo participants.

The *gi*, the official costume of judo, is one formal part of the sport. Consisting of a jacket made of strong cotton material and loose cotton trousers that generally extend below the knees to prevent scrapes on the hard springy mats, the *gi* serves a practical purpose in judo. The jacket has strong collars and lapels to resist the tugs and pulls of your opponent. There are no snaps or buttons on the *gi*, so that accidental damage may be prevented. A belt is always worn, and it is wrapped twice around the waist and tied in the middle with a square knot. Judo players compete in their bare feet.

Common sense and unwritten law dictate that a judo player wear a clean *gi* and keep toenails and fingernails short, to avoid scratching an opponent. Kicking, hitting, or gouging an opponent is not permitted.

The judo bow is a major form of etiquette. You have seen how boxers and wrestlers shake hands before a match. In judo, the bow, in effect, serves as the handshake.

Contestants begin by squatting as they face each other from a position about three feet apart on the mat. Heels are placed under buttocks. Palms are placed in front of both knees. Fingertips are turned slightly inward. Elbows are bent. The head is slightly lowered to shoulder level. Then there is a slight raising of the upper body. The contestants stand. The match begins. When the competition is finished, the same procedure is followed.

An area of about two hundred square feet is needed for a pair of judo contestants. Matches are won when a player is awarded points for throwing an opponent clearly to the ground or paralyzing an opponent for a set time, or when a player forces an opponent to surrender.

Instructors are always respected. Assistance in training for the sport is always given to beginners by even the most accomplished judo experts—for they remember they too were once beginners.

JUDO RANKS

Kodokan College in Tokyo establishes and supervises judo rules all over the world. The grading system is symbolized by the belts worn by judo participants *(judoka)*. Grades are divided into degree *(Dan)* and pupil *(Kyu)* selections. Fighting ability and technical skills determine the grades. To move above the rank of fifth *Dan*, the *judoka* is graded on impact on and contributions to the sport. Only a handful of men have achieved the rank of tenth *Dan*, and all were Japanese.

Beginners in judo all wear white belts. The following progression is then in effect:

Senior (over 17 years)		Junior (under 17 years)	
Yellow	5th *Kyu*	Yellow	5th *Kyu*
Green	4th *Kyu*	Orange	4th *Kyu*
Brown	3rd *Kyu*	Green	3rd *Kyu*
Brown	2nd *Kyu*	Blue	2nd *Kyu*
Brown (Advanced)	1st *Kyu*	Purple	1st *Kyu*

After one attains the rating of first *Kyu*, he hopefully will move upward, progressing through the ranks of *Dan*. First through fifth *Dan* wear black belts. Sixth through eighth *Dan* wear red and white belts. Ninth through eleventh *Dan* wear red. The white belt of the twelfth *Dan* has only been awarded once. Dr. Jigoro Kano was the only person to attain this rank and come virtually full circle, colorwise, in judo. The twelfth *Dan* white belt is twice as wide as the white belt of the beginner.

JUDO AND YOUR BODY

Since a big part of the sport is the balancing of your own body and the unbalancing of the body of your opponent, it is very important that you learn the natural judo stance, the self-defense position, the judo hold, and the judo walk.

THE NATURAL STANCE

Easy to assume and providing little fatigue, the natural stance is one of the keys to effective judo. You face your opponent with your weight equally distributed on both legs, which are spread slightly apart. You should allow your arms to hang loosely at your sides. Relax your shoulders and your knees. Keep your back straight and your chest out. Tense your abdomen, which is the focus of strength, but don't suck in too much air, and keep your lips sealed. In this most natural of positions, you can easily move to the side, step forward, or move back.

Variations of the natural stance are the right natural stance and the left natural stance. The only major changes are in how you place your feet. In the right natural stance, you bring your right foot forward and your left heel is moved slightly inward. In the left natural stance, bring the left foot slightly forward about one step and turn your right heel slightly inward. In both of these variations of the natural stance, you still keep your weight equally balanced on both feet, with your chin pulled in and your eyes straight ahead, as if focusing on a large object in front of you.

THE SELF-DEFENSE POSITION

The self-defense position is basically another variation from the natural stance. Your feet are placed about twelve inches apart and your knees are bent. You lower the upper part of your body. By placing your right foot forward, you get into the right self-defense position. Placing your left foot forward switches you into the left self-defense position.

THE JUDO WALK

It is easy to spot a person trained in judo by noting the way he or she walks. A judo player stands with feet spread slightly apart, weight equally distributed, knees slightly bent. Movement comes from the hips, for the hips and the abdomen are where real strength comes from. When you move across the mat, take pains to walk with short, sliding steps. Keep your balance low and don't get your feet crossed as you move—or you may find that not only your feet get crossed up.

THE JUDO HOLD

Development of the judo hold will help you to reduce injuries and progress quicker in the sport. Whether in free play or fighting practice *(Randori)*, form practice *(Kata)*, or competition *(Shiai)*, the same principles apply. Lightly grip the left lapel of your opponent's jacket with your right hand. Your left hand should grip your opponent's right outer sleeve at just about the midpoint between the elbow and the wrist. Your partner should do the same thing to you. As soon as both of you are comfortable, move about and try to unbalance each other. Continue grasping and continue the unbalancing attempts.

The trick involved in this outgrowth of the judo hold is for you to discover how to hold your own balance and break or disturb your partner's or opponent's balance or posture. This is called *Tsukuri*.

A beginner in judo should spend many hours getting the feel of *Tsukuri* with different partners or opponents. You will not be able to succeed in throwing an opponent unless you become skilled in *Tsukuri*. A couple of good

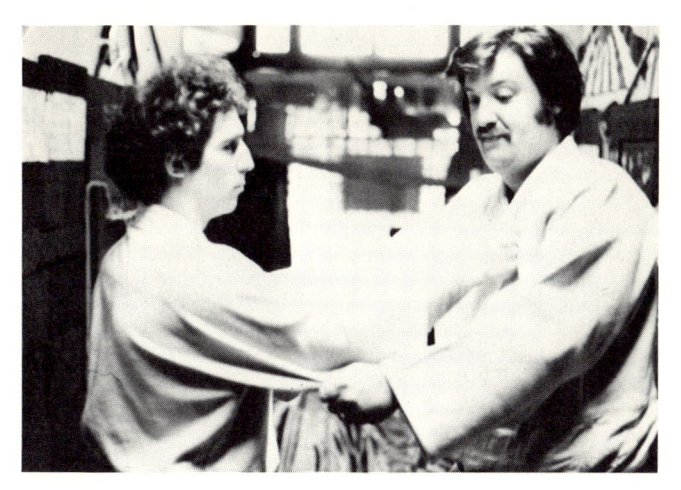

The Judo Hold: hand placement—right hand grips left lapel of opponent's jacket; left hand grips opponent's right outer sleeve.

Judo Hold: balance helps the hold.

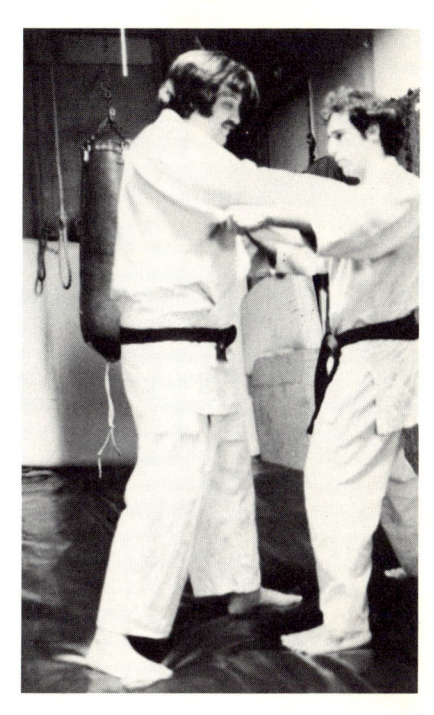

Tsukuri: *attempting to unbalance an opponent.*

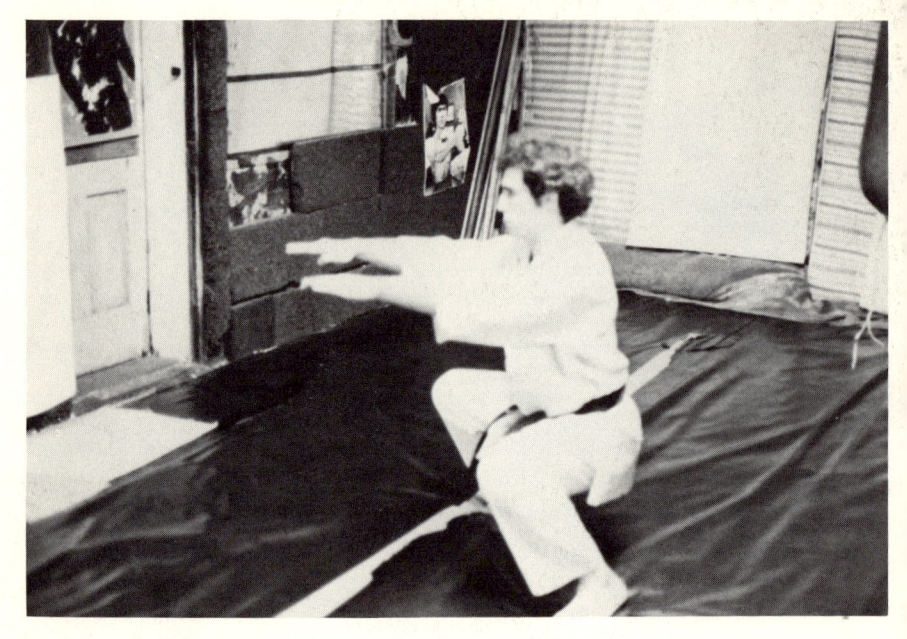

Breakfall (Ukemi): *squatting in preparation for breakfall.*

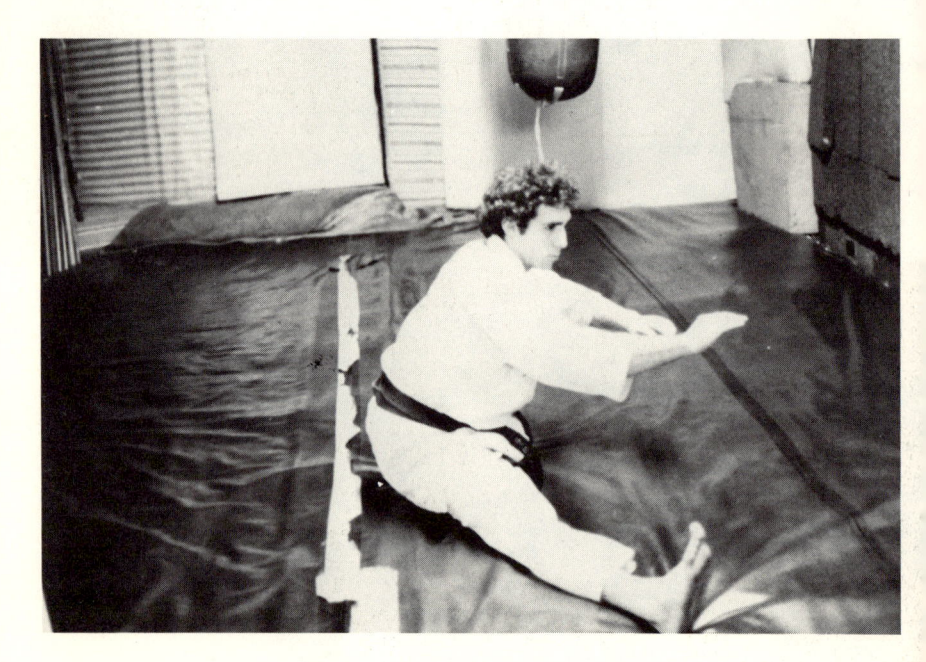

Ukemi: *poised for side breakfall.*

Ukemi: *side-breakfall hand position—right arm moves naturally across the body.*

Ukemi: *side breakfall end-point.*

Ukemi: *backward breakfall—at end-point legs automatically come up.*

tips to bear in mind: Don't raise your elbows too much and never lift your feet too much from the mat.

BREAKFALLS (UKEMI)

Judo is a sport with a lot of ups and a lot of downs. To go down, you'll have to fall, and knowing how to fall is a very important part of the sport for a beginner. Damaged pride and sometimes a damaged body can be avoided if you prepare yourself for a fall and learn how to cushion it. Practice breakfalls until they become automatic. There are three basic categories of breakfalls: falling backward, sideways, and forward.

BACKWARD BREAKFALLS *(Koho Ukemi)*

Get into a seated position on a mat or mattress. Put your arms out in front of you at shoulder height. Next, either cross your arms over your chest or keep them extended with your palms down and your fingers extended. Roll back onto your shoulders. Your legs will pop up automatically. Slap the mat hard with both palms and the back of your forearms the instant your back touches the mat. This is the slap that breaks the fall.

Remember to stare at your belt as you fall back and to keep your chin tucked in. This will prevent you from striking your head on the mat. Remember to create an angle of 30–45 degrees with your arms—don't keep them straight out. The proper angle helps you in your roll and is useful in the cushioning of the impact.

Variations of the backward breakfall include performing it from a squatting and then a standing position. Apply the same principles as those applicable to the seated position.

From the squatting position, lower yourself by doing a knee-bend with your left leg. Slap the mat with your right hand and the upper part of your right forearm. You can reverse the procedure by lowering your right leg and slapping the mat with your left hand and forearm.

The breakfall backward from the standing position follows very much the same procedure. Since the fall is from a greater distance, even more relaxation and protection of the head is needed. Move back one or two steps. Go down as if you are doing a knee-bend. Sit on the mat. Roll. As in the other backward breakfalls, your legs will automatically come up. Follow the same procedure as with the seated breakfall.

Remember: head up, chin tucked in, practice and relax, relax and practice. Get it right for all the hundreds of ups and downs and falls you'll have in judo.

SIDE BREAKFALLS *(O-Ho-Ukemi)*

Lie down on your back on the mat. Raise your legs and roll to the right side. Slap the mat with your right hand and forearm only. Your left arm should move naturally across your body. Remember to keep your chin tucked in. This will help protect your neck and head. Repeat the procedure rolling to the left side.

Next, practice the side breakfall from a sitting position. Put your right arm out in front of you. Place your left arm over your stomach. Keep this arm relaxed. Bending your elbow, bring your right arm in and across your chest. Your right palm should face downward. Fall back. Twist your body to the right. Slap the mat with your right hand and forearm. Repeat this procedure from the left side.

After you have mastered the side breakfall from a prone position and from a seated position, you should be ready to do it from a crouch and finally from a standing position. The basic moves from a crouch position begin with squatting and in one motion putting your right leg forward and your right arm across your chest. Roll backward and twist slightly to the right. Keep your head and chin up. Slap the mat with your right palm and forearm. Repeat the procedure from the other side. Once you have done the crouching side breakfall dozens of times and have picked up speed and timing and feel comfortable, you will be ready for the side breakfall from a standing position.

With your feet almost together, stand in as relaxed a position as possible. Place your left foot about a step to the left and point it outward. Then lift your right foot just a bit off the mat. At this time, your right arm should be brought across your body.

Move your right arm and leg in the same motion and lower your body to the mat. Sit. Roll backward and twist to the right. The same slapping of the mat with your right hand and under forearm, the same natural coming up of your legs, the same tucked-in-chin and head-up principles apply.

Practice this standing breakfall from the left side. After many practices from the left and the right sides, you'll find that you'll be able to fall very naturally with no fear and with ease. Once again, since judo involves so much falling, it is very, very important that you put the practice time into the breakfalls.

FORWARD BREAKFALL *(Zenpo Ukemi)*

In some ways the forward break- or tumblefall is like a somersault, but there are some very important differences. Some experts can do the forward breakfall over such obstacles as tables or chairs without even touching them. The forward breakfall is more difficult to do than the back or the side breakfalls, but it is a great conditioner and builder of confidence.

Place your right foot a little forward. Bend and place your right hand between your legs. Your fingers should point inward. Your left hand should rest gently on the mat in front of your left foot. Now lower yourself and in one motion make the back part of your head and your right shoulder touch the mat. Roll forward sharply, using your legs and waist for drive. Keep the lead shoulder tucked in so that it does not hit the mat.

As you come near the end of the roll, beat the mat with your left hand and the underpart of your forearm. Do this with as much power as possible. After you do this time after time, you will notice that the momentum of the roll and the beating will help to bring you to your feet.

Remember that the roll-out succeeds because of the momentum you build up. The roll-out depends on the body being kept in a circular shape from the start of the roll to the completion of the roll.

Ukemi provides confidence. Only through practice, starting from slow and low levels and then building to higher and faster levels of falls, will you as a *judoka* be able to move into competition having some faith in your ability to hold your own against an opponent, or at least to wind up unhurt. Practice!

THROWING TECHNIQUES (NAGE WAZA)

The heart of judo—the ability to compete without fear of physical injury—is what throwing techniques are all about. Throwing techniques vary from the most simple to the very complex, from the most dramatic to the very basic. Key points concerning the techniques of throwing include:

1. Anticipate. Mental preparation for judo involves anticipating the moves of your opponent and planning

ahead in your own mind what you will do. Watch how your opponent distributes his weight. If you can break his balance *(kuzushi),* you can throw him. By pushing or pulling, balance can be broken. Remember that if you can get an opponent on his toes or heels, he can't attack very efficiently.

2. Guard your body. You will be attempting to unbalance your opponent. You will also be striving to maintain your own balance. Guard your balance and stay relaxed. If you tense your muscles, the speed, timing, and agility needed for judo throwing techniques are handicapped.

3. Don't waste energy. You can conserve your strength by off-balancing your opponent. Off-balancing is much more effective than strength versus strength. Resist your opponent and get him to exert effort. In that way, you will be getting him to use strength, while you will use that strength against him.

4. Use abdominal breathing as an aid in the development of strength and endurance. Tension in the abdominal muscles provides power.

5. Grip your opponent properly. You should never grip your opponent's jacket too tightly or stiffen your arm too much until you move into the throw; otherwise, you'll get fatigued too quickly. A normal and effective grip consists of placing your fingers on the outside and your thumb on the inside of the lapel of your opponent's jacket. The *reverse grip* position is thumb outside and fingers inside the lapel.

6. Throw your opponent properly. Always throw him

in the direction in which he's moving. For example, a player leaning backward should be thrown backward.

7. Time your throw carefully. An opponent stepping backward or forward, to the left or to the right, is in an ideal position for you to time your throw. In many ways, *when* you make your move is nearly as important as *how* you make your move.

8. The thrower *(tori)* is responsible for the one who is thrown *(uke)*. Always make your moves with care, for there is danger in the rough execution of throws. When you practice, be concerned with accuracy, not speed. Speed will come with the practice of accuracy. The *tori* should allow the *uke* the opportunity to get up. If you stand back a bit, this will help you avoid the *uke*'s immediate counterattack. If you are in the role of the *uke*, rise from your thrown position facing the *tori*. Bend your left arm upward to help fend off an attack as you rise.

TYPES OF THROWS

The hundreds of variations of throws have given judo worldwide popularity. The suddenness, the dramatic skill, and the physical dexterity throws seem to involve contribute to judo's mystique. Yet there is really no secret to the proper performance of throws; they all share the same basic principles of balance, leverage, and timing.

Each throwing technique is related to a different part

of the thrower's body. This section will explain four basic categories of judo throws: foot throws, strong take-down techniques carrying the element of surprise when either the leg or the foot sweeps the opponent to the mat; hip throws, in which the player jams his hip into his opponent and spins the opponent over the top or side; hand throws, in which strong hand-and-arm movements coordinate with the shoulders for throwing; and stomach throws, in effect sacrifice throws, in which you maneuver yourself to the ground and pull down your opponent.

Foot and Leg Techniques (Ashi Waza)

MAJOR OUTSIDE LEG THROW (Osoto Gari)

Perhaps the easiest of all judo throws to learn and perform, *osoto gari* gets your opponent on one leg, unbalances him, and sweeps him off his feet.

From the right natural stance move out on your left foot. Position it outside your opponent's right foot. Bend your left knee slightly. Push with your right forearm and hand from your opponent's collarbone down to the right rear. Pull with power with your left hand and get your opponent's right sleeve anchored into your left armpit. Swing your right leg forward, bending your right knee and sweeping it to the back of your opponent's right knee. Make contact as high up above his knee as possible and sweep away the support of his right leg. At the

Major Outside Leg Throw (Osoto Gari): sweeping away support—front view.

Osoto Gari: *sweeping away support—back view.*

Osoto Gari: *pointing head and right foot at the mat helps force opponent off balance.*

moment you do this, reverse your right-arm pressure. Use your arm as a lever and push back and up against the neck of your opponent. Point your head and your right foot at the mat. These movements will combine with the force of your leg and right arm to dash your opponent to the mat.

All the actions should flow simultaneously. Remember to bend your upper body forward as you sweep your opponent off his feet. Finally, relax your left pulling-hand until the throw is completed.

MAJOR INSIDE REAP *(Ouchi Gari)*

A basic leg-and-foot throw to force your opponent onto his back, *ouchi gari* works well for any-size judo player. It works especially well against an opponent who operates defensively.

With your feet spread wide and operating out of a right natural stance, use your right hand to push the left side of your opponent's chest toward his left rear. Your left hand should control your opponent's right arm by pulling down on it. Get your right foot forward between your opponent's feet. Lean your left foot left, with the knee bent slightly. The heel of your right foot should lock your left foot in a hook.

Now swing your right foot with the right heel out and reap (sweep) your opponent's extreme lower calf. The pressure of your left knee extension, your right hand

Major Inside Reap (Ouchi Gari): *push-pull effect in operation; left hand pulls, right hand pushes while right leg reaps opponent's lower calf.*

pushing back and downward, and your left hand pulling on his sleeve should all combine to down him.

Coordination is essential in the proper performance of the move: your right foot reaps, your left hand pulls, your right hand pushes. Both you and your opponent, in effect, are hopping on one foot, except that you have his foot locked and he's hopping backward. Don't make the mistake of many beginners and slacken your attack if there is resistance. Give more pressure. Reap, pull, push, pin!

MINOR OUTSIDE REAP *(Kosoto Gari)*

This fairly simple foot throw is used when your opponent moves his right foot forward and is about to plant his body weight on that foot. You reap with your left foot at the *outside* of your opponent's right heel. Timing is the key element in this move, which is a classic example of how judo allows you to use just enough power to do what you have to with an opponent.

If you see your opponent move forward on his left foot, set him up for *kosoto gari* by moving to the side with your right foot and angling and lifting your left foot to the side. Your opponent will now begin to move his right foot forward and prepare to put body weight on that foot. At this instant, slap with your left foot. Get power into the sole of your foot, for this is the surface that will strike the outside of your opponent's right heel.

Coordinate this reaping with the proper hand move-

Minor Outside Reap (Kosoto Gari): *reaping with left foot at outside of opponent's right heel. Push-pull effect of left and right hand again in operation.*

ments. Pull straight down with your left hand to get your opponent's right arm to his right front. Push to your opponent's right with your right hand. Off-balance him to clinch the reap by switching the direction of your right hand and pushing him toward his right rear.

There are a couple of key points to remember: Don't turn your ankle up when you reap, but get your toes inward and your whole foot into the move; and keep your balance by supporting yourself on the ball of your right foot.

Mastery of *kosoto gari* should set you up nicely for the Minor Outside Hook *(Kosoto Gake)*. The basic difference between the two moves is that most often *kosoto gake* is used when your opponent's right foot is back, while in *kosoto gari* the right foot is forward.

MINOR INSIDE REAP *(Kouchi Gari)*

This foot technique has many advantages: a smaller person can rack up a bigger person in an instant; it is an excellent move to use as a feint followed up with a hip throw; and there are many situations where you will be able to put the move into play. The different parts that make up *kouchi gari* are relatively simple. The only drawback to this move is that you must perfect timing and smooth body movement—and this takes much, much practice.

From the right natural stance, get your opponent to move forward with his right foot. Just at the moment he

Minor Inside Reap (Kouchi Gari): *good foot technique—off-balancing to the right and rear.*

is about to place that foot on the mat, off-balance him towards his right rear.

Get the bottom of your left foot, with the toes pointing left, directly *behind* your opponent's right heel. Reap his heel toward his toes. Pull his right sleeve straight down with your left hand. Use your right hand to push him toward his right rear and onto his back.

The move is simple—you force him onto one leg and then sweep that leg out from under him. Note that the more weight your opponent places on his heel, the easier is the reaping for you. The more of your body you can get into the throw, the more powerful will be the throw. The more exact the timing of the move, the more effective will the move be. Reap the instant his right foot is about to be placed on the mat.

RETREATING FOOT SWEEP *(Okuri Ashi Barai)*

This foot throw is considered easy to perform, since it does not require great force on your part and its movements are easy to understand. Yet it is difficult to execute well unless you are prepared to put in many hours of practice to get your timing and flow perfected. Once you have done this, you'll be able to triumph over any-size opponent. Fine for offense, *okuri ashi barai* can be used when another of your throw attempts has been frustrated. This retreating foot-sweep works well from either side; therefore, it's recommended that you practice using both your left and right feet.

Retreating Foot Sweep (Okuri Ashi Barai): *getting the whole body into the throw.*

Okuri Ashi Barai: *easing opponent down with care, you want to subdue but not damage your partner.*

Move into position directly to the right of your opponent, getting him to move to his left. When you see him move his left foot to the side, lift him up and to the left side with your right hand. Then get your opponent off-balanced to the right side for a moment by pressing your left hand into his right armpit area. As this is done, position your right foot slightly to the inside and in front of his feet.

These maneuvers should get your opponent to shift his body weight onto his right foot. Get your right foot in front of his left and apply the sole of your left foot to his right ankle. (You should be directly in front of his body at this point.) His right foot movement signals your sweep—sweep his right foot in the direction in which he moves. Pull downward with your left hand on his right sleeve; push upward with your right hand.

The secret of this "foot slap" move is to time your foot contact with hand-and-arm movement and sweeping. Get your whole body into the throw, not just your legs.

INSIDE THIGH THROW *(Uchi Mata)*

This technique works well against an opponent who has his legs spread wide apart. It's also effective if you are taller than your opponent and thus able to get body leverage to work in your favor.

Get a good grip and start the *uchi mata* by picking up your left foot. Pivot on your right foot. Thrust your left

Inside Thigh Throw (Uchi Mata): *height advantage over an opponent and his legs spread wide gives edge to thrower.*

Uchi Mata: *leg leverage sweeps inside of opponent's thigh.*

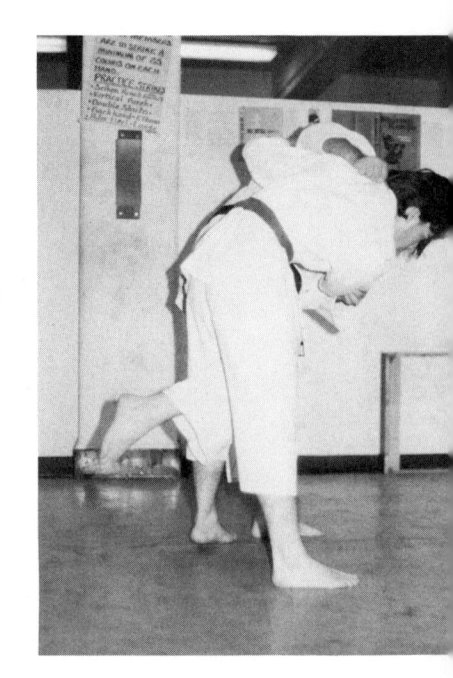

foot deep between the legs of your opponent. Get as deep as possible to avoid injuring his groin. Brace your right foot, which supports both bodies.

Use your hands and arms to pull your opponent onto your hip as you straighten your left foot and sweep it up and against your opponent. The leverage of your leg sweeping up against the inside of his thigh and your hip action will lift him off the ground, over and onto the mat. You actually throw by pulling around and down with your left hand, and forward and up with your right hand. Hold his right sleeve firmly as you perform the throw.

A couple of special points to remember: As your opponent starts to fall, aim your forehead at the mat to aid your concentration and follow-through; pull strongly with both hands to raise your opponent's gravity center; and point the toes of your right foot to the right to get added balance and support.

Finally, these *key principles for all leg throws* are worth stressing:

1. All foot and leg movement should be done with a purpose. Violence and wildness have no place in these throws.

2. Timing is crucial. Continuous practice is needed for you to get the timing down to the point where it becomes almost automatic.

3. All of your movements must flow. You should strive to master simultaneous movements, including sweeping and pinning.

4. The role of your hands and your body in leg throws (and all throws) is very important. Unbalancing, the heart all of throwing, comes from the intelligent use of your hands and your body.

5. The sole of your foot should be used in these throws as often as possible. The sole of your foot can take punishment and thus will reduce pain for you. The sole also gets your body properly positioned for throwing.

Hip Techniques (Koshi Waza)

FLOATING HIP THROW *(Uki Goshi)*

This hip throw is very important for you to learn, because it is the basis for many other hip techniques. Once you master the mechanical leverage of *uki goshi,* you will be able to apply it to other moves.

Begin by standing sideways to your opponent—your right side should be placed in close contact with the chest and stomach of your opponent. Your knees are slightly bent, your belt is below his, your right hip juts into him slightly.

Pass your right arm around your opponent's waist and concentrate his weight against you. Pull his right sleeve parallel to the ground with your left hand. Lift up with your right hand. Now switch your weight to your left foot. You'll raise your opponent on his toes. A deliberate move of your head and body to the left and your left hand placed near his left armpit will send your opponent over your right hip, and you'll be able to throw him.

The throw is effectively performed if you rotate and twist your hips. You don't lift your opponent onto your hips or back. Always arch your back when you position your hips. Always keep close body contact throughout the stages of the throw, or else you won't be able to get the proper leverage.

Since *uki goshi* is the basis for most hip throws, you should practice it in stages to perfect your technique: position yourself, get the proper grips, transfer your weight, turn your body and head, twist your opponent over your hip.

MAJOR HIP THROW *(Ogoshi)*

Another basic hip throw, this move resembles *uki goshi*. The major difference is that in *ogoshi* you lift the whole front of your opponent's body onto your back, whereas *uki goshi* relies on you twisting your hip.

Lead with your right foot, positioning it slightly outside of the left foot of your opponent. Pivot on your right foot and position your left foot inside your opponent's left foot. Get in there deep. You unweight your opponent by reaching around his waist with your right hand and using your left hand to pull his right arm up and out.

Snap your legs to straighten them in order to get more power into your lift. Your opponent should come over

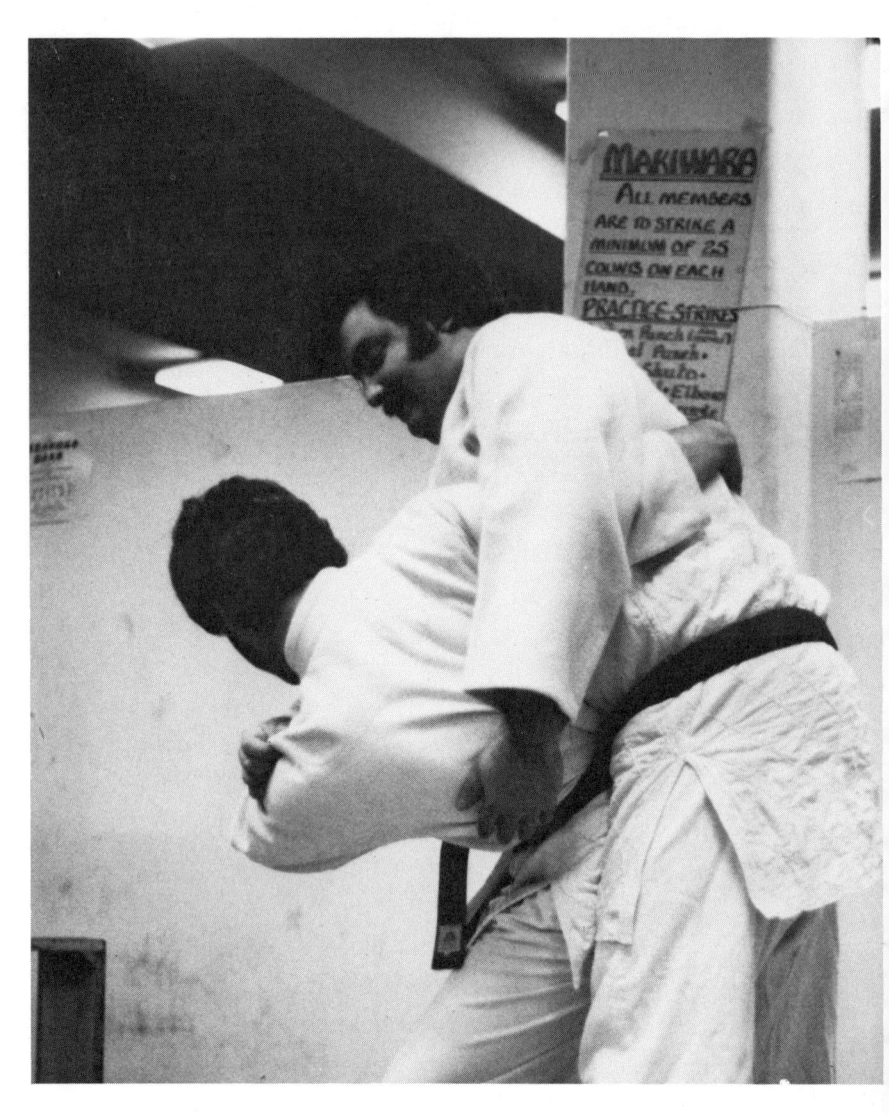

Major Hip Throw (Ogoshi): *getting in deep helps focus force for the throw.*

your right shoulder, over your hips, and into a horizontal plane in front of you.

Some key things to bear in mind in executing the throw are to get your left foot inside your opponent's left foot as you position your hips, to pull forward strongly with your hands when your opponent is on your back, and to remember that leverage and lifting come from hip power, so get a lot into it.

SWEEPING HIP THROW (Harai Goshi)

Professor Kano developed this throw for use against an adversary who jumped to the front to frustrate the *uki goshi*. Footwork and timing are very important parts of the *harai goshi*.

Step forward and pivot on your left foot. Get your right leg off the ground and sweep your opponent's legs out from under him. Swing your whole leg loosely so that there is contact between your thigh and that of your opponent.

You should pull with power with your left hand, which grips your opponent's right arm at shoulder level; pull with your upper body tilted toward the left rear. Get your right elbow and forearm below the left armpit of your opponent to lower his center of gravity.

As you throw, rotate your body to the left and get more power by rotating your head to the left and tucking in your chin.

JUDO: THE "GENTLE" SPORT

Springing Hip Throw (Hane Goshi): *the hip is the springboard for the thro along with body rotation.*

SPRINGING HIP THROW *(Hane Goshi)*

You need some speed to perform this throw well. The force of the throw comes from the springing effect of your knee action, and you throw from the hip with your back arched.

Step in with one foot. Pivot. Get your other foot deep inside the legs of your opponent with a whirling and springing motion. Sweep the leg of your opponent out and pull him onto your hip; then use your arms to lift and drop your opponent.

Get as much of the material of your opponent's *gi* as possible by pulling with power with both hands. The leg you use to contact the inner part of your opponent's leg should bend slightly at the knee. Your hip is the springboard for the throw, along with your body rotation. Note that by straightening your left knee, you spring your opponent upward with the back of your hips. By rotating your body to the left, you make the throw over your right hip, downward and to the front.

Finally, these *key principles for all hip throws* are worth stressing:

1. Smooth, flowing moves are best for all hip throws. These will help your timing and not tip off your moves to your opponent.

2. Strive always for close body contact in order to get the leverage needed. If you have too much space between you and your opponent, think seriously about another throw.

3. Speed and power must come from your hands. The throw comes from the hip, but the guiding control comes from what you do with your hands. However, the whole body must turn continuously, even though you pull with your hands.

4. Remember to keep on going once you are turning your opponent into a hip throw. If you pause, you give an edge to your opponent. Keep your momentum and force building into the throw.

5. All hip throws require that you arch your back.

Hand Techniques (Te Waza)

THE SHOULDER THROW *(Ippon Seoi Nage)*

This is a spectacular hand throw that is especially effective when used by a smaller player against a taller adversary. Speed is an important factor in the success of the throw, for you have to be "on" your opponent before he can react and block you. You must also use your hands and your hip precisely and powerfully.

Grip the inside of your opponent's right sleeve. Start moving his right arm up and forward. Use both your hands. Now step and pivot into him on your lead foot. Place your other foot between his legs. Relax your right-hand grip and move your right arm under your opponent's right armpit. The back of your shoulders and your back should make tight contact against his body. Lock his right arm in place by using the bend of your right elbow like a lever.

Straighten your hip and knees. He'll come up on your back. Bend your upper body forward. Pull down and forward with power with both hands. Your opponent will be lifted past your shoulders and be thrown to the front.

Note that the throw should come off your toes and not your heels. Get your shoulder deep into your opponent. If there is resistance to the throw, drop on one knee for more leverage.

Shoulder Throw (Ippon Seoi Nage): *especially effective when used by a smaller opponent against a larger adversary.*

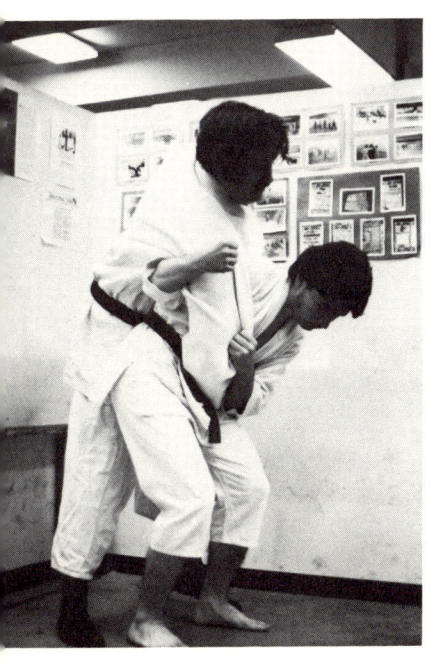

Ippon Seoi Nage: *back of shoulder and back make firm contact with opponent's body.*

This move is very similar to the basic *ippon seoi nage* except that your hands and arms are used in very different ways. You pull at your opponent's right sleeve with your left hand and at the same time get your right hand to twist into his lapel. As you twist and pull his arm forward, you get leverage as your right elbow slides into your opponent's left armpit. Completion of the throw depends on you pulling as hard as you can, using both arms.

Floating Drop (Uki Otoshi): *opponent has been thrown and dropped—end-point.*

FLOATING DROP *(Uki Otoshi)*

This hand technique is the first of a series of fifteen fundamental throws called the *nage-no-kata*. If you master *uki otoshi,* you will learn at the same time effective body movement and body distribution and efficient gripping methods and posture, and you will also gain insights into strength and off-balancing techniques.

Step back from your opponent and position your right foot diagonally, about eighteen inches from your right rear. Push with your right hand at your opponent's left jawbone. Pull upward on your opponent's right sleeve with your left hand.

Lean your body back so that it is elevated on your right foot, drawing your opponent forward on his right foot. Now drop quickly but smoothly to your left knee. By pulling down with both your hands, you'll be able to turn your opponent and throw him to your left rear.

Sacrifice Techniques (Utemi Waza)

STOMACH THROW *(Tomoe Nage)*

A dramatic throw that has been much publicized in films and television programs, the *tomoe nage* allows you to really rack up an opponent who comes charging in at you. It is classified as a rear sacrifice throw. If you do

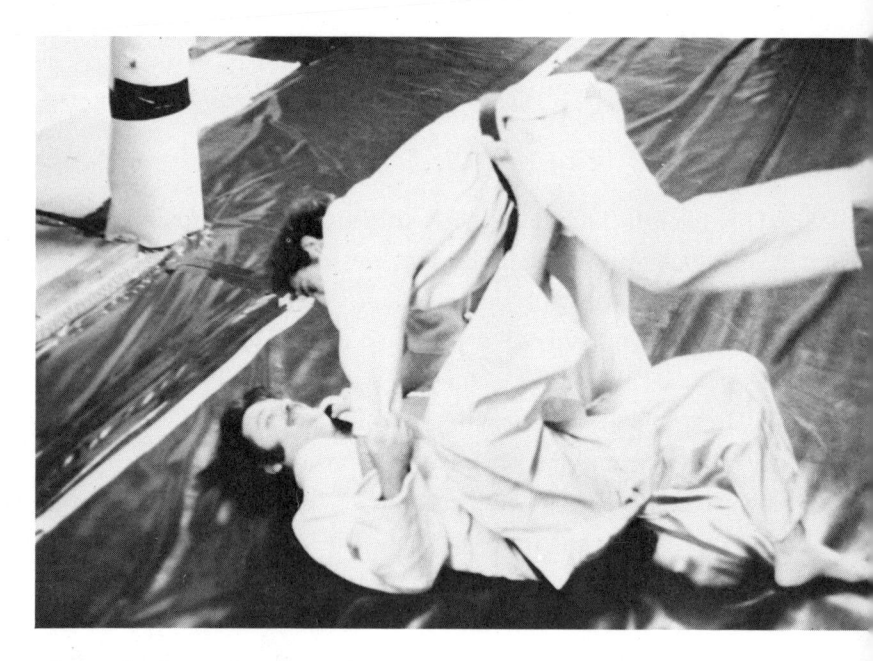

Stomach Throw (Tomoe Nage): *opponent goes hurtling over the shoulder after being lifted with the sole of the foot.*

not execute *tomoe nage* properly, you are left in an awkward and nondefensible position—thus the term "sacrifice throw." *Tomoe nage* is effective in that you can give way to the aggressive pushing of an opponent and then turn his strength against him. Beginning students are cautioned to learn this throw in stages and in slow motion to avoid injuries.

Move in close to your opponent who is pressing you. Grab his lapels and lift so that you get him on his toes. Position your left foot between his legs and fall down, getting onto your back. As you do this, raise your right

JUDO: THE "GENTLE" SPORT

leg and position the sole of your right foot on your opponent's stomach.

Your opponent should be positioned directly over you. Roll back on your shoulders and push your right leg deeper into his stomach—the lifting surface is the sole of your foot. Turn your wrists up and lift with your hands, which have a powerful grip on his lapels. The result of all these actions should be to send your opponent hurtling over your shoulder to land hard on his back.

There are several key things to remember. Don't push too soon, or your foot pressure will keep your opponent up. Push when your body and his are positioned properly, as described. Your grip on his lapels is important. Hold on hard and get a lot of material. Coordinate pulling his lapels with bending your knees and lifting your right leg. You should move into the throw by rolling back on the mat, lowering your buttocks in a sliding manner. Don't just drop down, as you may hurt yourself.

SACRIFICE THROW *(Maki Komi)*

This move causes you, in effect, to surrender position to your opponent. However, the suddenness and power of the move help you prevail.

From the normal stance and hold, move your left foot back and pull your opponent's arm forward with your left hand. Get your right arm across his chest and grip his right arm tightly and control it. Bend your knees and lower your body at this point. Seal off his right side by

Sacrifice Throw (Maki Komi): *left hand grips and controls opponent's right arm, knees begin to bend and body is lowered in preparation for throw.*

positioning your right foot outside his right foot. Start pivoting your body to the left. Straighten your legs. Lift him off the ground. Positioning your right hand on the ground, fall at the side of your opponent and roll to the right. You will now be able to swing your opponent over your body to make your hold-down.

There are literally hundreds of throws. Descriptions of these could fill two more books this size. The basic throws have been presented here, however, and they are more than enough to get you started in judo.

Most *judoka*s find it best to concentrate on one or two throws that they find most comfortable for their bodies and personalities. Experts do the same thing, calling these throws their "pet throws."

Short persons generally do best with a hip throw; sometimes a shoulder throw is satisfactory. Foot or leg throws most often work best for taller players. You should practice your pet throw thousands of times until you get it perfect. Then move on to another and then another throw.

HOLD-DOWNS (OSAE KOMI WAZA)

Once you have taken down an opponent through one of the throws explained in the previous section, your aim is then to subdue that person on the mat through a hold-down. You can force him into saying the magic word *mattai* ("I give up"), or you can get him or her to tap twice or more with either hand or foot on your body or his. If this is not possible, the mat can be tapped.

One full point (an *ippon*) is awarded for a thirty-second hold-down. A half-point (a *waza ari*) is given for a hold-down of twenty-five seconds or more but less than thirty seconds. A score of two half-points (a *wazari awasete ippon*) is achieved by getting two consecutive *waza aris*.

Effective mat technique involves using all your body weight and keeping your center of gravity very low. Flexibility, especially in your limbs, is very important. Rigid limbs hamper quick movement and reaction flow. You should exert maximum strength when your opponent is not able to let out all of his or her power. For example, your adversary is at his strongest during the first escape attempt. Once the escape moves are in progress, your opponent is at his weakest. Over-balance at that time. Using the laws of physics as a guide, get your weight down to the area of the body your opponent will try to use as an escape route.

No hold is a poor hold if you bear in mind that all holds serve to tire out the man underneath; if your hold is being broken, give it up and move on to another hold.

SCARF HOLD *(Kesa Gatame)*

An excellent hold-down technique for beginners, ef-

Scarf Hold (Kesa Gatame): *notice how the full weight of the thrower and his arm around the neck of the opponent operate to make for an excellent hold-down.*

fective for smaller persons against larger opponents, this hold begins once you get your opponent on his back. Approach from a right angle. Grasp his right arm above the elbow. Control that arm by pinning it under your left armpit. Spread your legs wide for stability and power. Open your stance to the left. Press your right side against your opponent's right side.

Now get your arm around his neck. Get a grip behind his collar with your thumb on the inside. You can push down from this position on the back of the collar if he tries to get his head up.

The final stage of the hold-down involves your legs. Slightly bend your right leg. Position your right knee almost at the tip of your opponent's shoulder. Bend your left leg, and spread it to the rear. Get the inside of your left foot balanced on the mat. Weight, balance, and concentration for the hold-down should come from right palm on the mat, head bent left, chin tucked in. Get your whole body into the hold.

SHOULDER HOLD-DOWN *(Kata Gatame)*

This move is considered by many to be the strongest judo hold. You can effectively move into it off *kesa gatame*. Your opponent may attempt to push your head away or to elbow you when his arm comes up and across his body to get out of *kesa gatame*. At this moment, start *kata gatame*.

Grasp behind his outstretched arm with your hands and lock them. Your left palm should face up, your right palm should face down. Put your head to the floor and use the right side of your neck to push your opponent's right triceps to the right and down—at the same time squeezing his right arm into his neck. Twist your right knee into his right side. Get your left leg out to the side and brace it with your instep. All this pressure should make him give in. Finally, remember that the key to this shoulder hold-down is the tight locking of your opponent's right arm and head with your arms.

houlder Hold-Down (Kata Gatame): *the key to this shoulder hold-down is the ght locking of opponent's right arm and his head with thrower's arms.*

SIDE FOUR-CORNER HOLD-DOWN
(Yoko Shiho Gatame)

You operate in this simple and interesting hold like a heavy weight. Come in from the side at a right angle. With both knees on the mat, insteps down, hips low, knees spread wide, press your chest against your opponent's stomach. Get both knees into solid contact with the right side of his body. Reach between his legs with

Side Four-Corner Hold-Down (Yoko Shiho Gatame): *chest is pressed against opponent's stomach like a heavy weight.*

Yoko Shiho Gatame: *arms cradling opponent's body exert still more weight pressure.*

Yoko Shiho Gatame: *head lowered so that left cheek presses against stomach creates still more weight pressure and completes move.*

both hands and grab his belt momentarily. Then change to a grip on the left rear part of his collar with your left hand, to control the upper part of his body. Your left cheek against his stomach and clamped arms powerfully cradling him should complete the hold. By adjusting your leg and feet positions and bringing both ankles straight up, you will be able to frustrate escape efforts.

CHOKING TECHNIQUES (SHIME WAZA)

Choking is an effective and natural judo technique, even though it might appear to be distasteful and too violent to perform at first. You don't strangle your opponent—you simply apply pressure to the jugular vein, the windpipe, the side of the neck, the carotid arteries. Generally, the lapel and collar of the *gi* function as a gripping lever. In all your choking moves, be constantly sensitive and alert to the condition of your opponent.

SLIDING LAPEL CHOKE *(Okuri Eri Jime)*

This is the most effective of all choking techniques. Once you get the move down pat, all you really have to do is get behind your opponent, apply *okuri eri jime,* and you have him in a condition where he will have to yield.

Get one hand, with your thumb inside, across his throat and lock the *gi*'s lapel. Position your other hand under your opponent's arm and pull down on the opposite collar. The result of this move is that your oppo-

JUDO: THE "GENTLE" SPORT

Sliding Lapel Choke (Okuri Eri Jime): with hand across throat, thumb is locked under gi's lapel.

Okuri Eri Jime: *the power of the far-collar choke places opponent in a position where he has to yield.*

nent's collar is now wrapped around his neck, creating pressure at three points at the same time. This choke exerts much power and can be used from a variety of positions.

REVERSE CROSS-CHOKE *(Gyaku Juji Jime)*

A very popular choking technique, *gyaku juji jime*

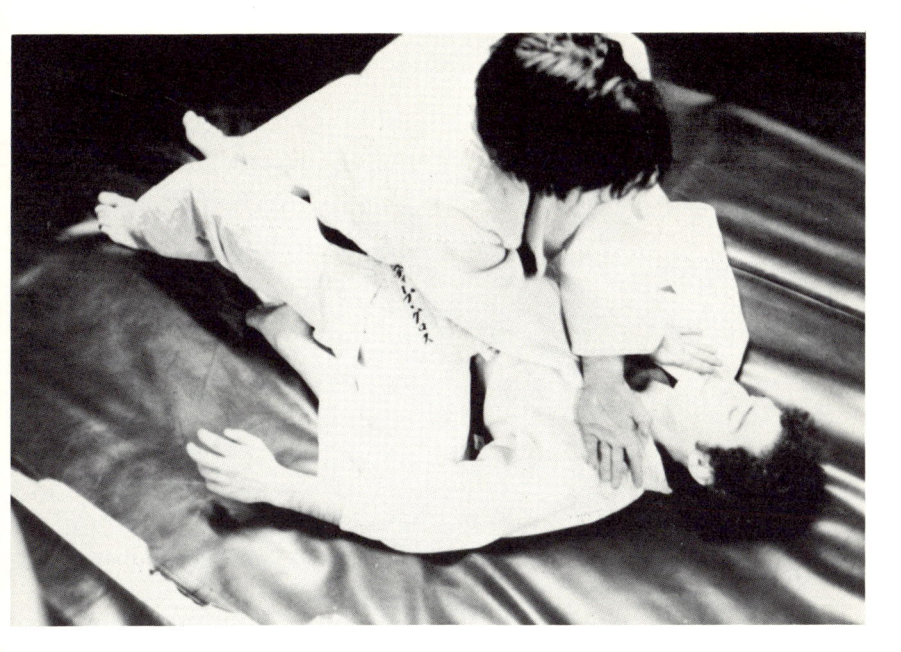

Reverse Cross-Choke (Gyaku Juji Jime): *hands are crossed and reach inside opponent's collar.*

Gyaku Juji Jime: *upraised arms of pinned player reveal force and power of choke.*

involves crossing your hands and reaching deep inside your opponent's collar. Your fingers should be on the inside, and your thumb should be on the outside. By bringing your hands together you move into the choke. *Gyaku juji jime* can be used whether you are on top or underneath your opponent.

HALF CROSS-CHOKE *(Kata Juji Jime)*

Seize your opponent's left collar with your left hand. Your thumb is positioned outside and your fingers inside the lapel. Get in deep. Press against the jugular vein with the joint of your thumb and forefinger. Cross over with your right hand, thumb inside and fingers outside the right lapel. Get deep again and grab a lot of material.

A twist to the left by your left hand will produce pressure from your thumb against your opponent's neck. Put your right wrist and forearm against his throat. Squeeze both hands tightly at the neck. You should get a tap out.

In the event you have an overactive opponent, his efforts can be lessened if you clamp his body tightly with your legs and feet. Lowering the upper part of your body can also bring more pressure to bear on him.

NAKED CHOKE *(Hadaka Jime)*

You do not use the *gi* in this move, and that's what gives it the name "naked choke." From a position be-

Naked Choke (Hadaka Jime): *right shoulder behind opponent's neck, and right cheek against left side of his face give this choke added control. Note the* gi *is not involved in this choke.*

hind your opponent, apply the right side of your wrist directly to his neck. Your right hand is placed across his throat. Get your left hand over his left shoulder. Clasp your palms together. Lean back and draw back on his throat. Your right shoulder behind his head and your right cheek against the left side of his face add further control.

The naked choke can be used in various ways: when you place one hand behind your opponent's head, when you are in front of your opponent, when you choke and he has his back on the mat.

Finally, in all choking movements keep the following pointers in mind:

1. Operate from a position where your moves are not restricted and where the moves of your opponent are able to be restricted.

2. Get the smaller sides of your wrists into the choke, much like wire or rope around your opponent's neck. Keep your wrists good and flexible.

ARMLOCK TECHNIQUES (KANSETSU WAZA)

Armlocks apply reverse pressure, or twisting motions, to the elbow. Excellent for self-defense, these armlocks can cause damage to the elbow, so be careful in performing them. In practice or competition, apply gradual pressure.

Unless caution is used, you'll do more to your opponent than just subdue him!

You should be able to move your own body about freely and yet have complete control over your opponent in applying *kansetsu waza*. Both speed and confidence are crucial in using armlocks efficiently. Wrist pressure on your opponent causes much pressure on his elbow, and this underscores the mechanical-lever principle that is so much a part of judo technique.

TWISTING ARM BAR WITH ARMPIT
(Waki Gatame)

This surprise move is perhaps the most media-publicized in all of judo. It's a good move to use when someone comes at you with an outstretched arm. It is also the most famous of the defenses against a knife attack.

Yank the outstretched arm quickly toward you and move to the side of your opponent. Your arm should go under and pin the outstretched arm. Get a hold on your opponent's other wrist and lock it. Bend his arm against his elbow. The leverage and pain and pressure that you create will quickly end the contest.

ARM BAR OVER CROSS-BODY *(Juji Gatame)*

This is a dramatic move that looks good and has devastating effects on an opponent when done well. You must

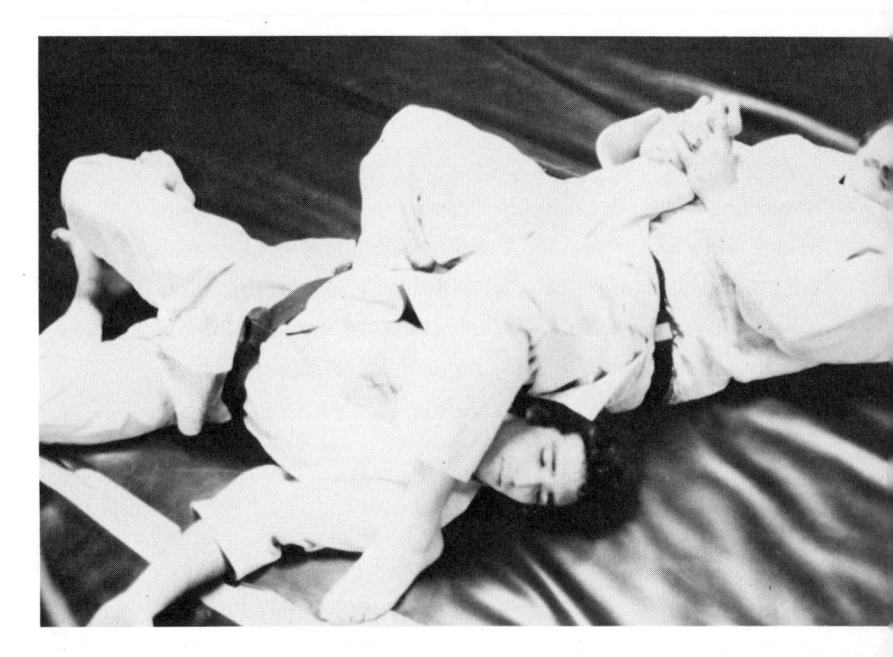

Arm Bar over Cross-Body (Juji Gatame): *opponent's arm is scissored with both legs, and both hands exert pressure on his wrist and elbow.*

get your body perpendicular to that of your adversary. Grabbing his wrist, scissor that arm with both your legs. Using both hands, twist the wrist to get lever pressure against his elbow, which you send in a rolling motion to the inside. If you can get your opponent onto his stomach, you'll be able to exert the greatest control for *juji gatame.*

The name "arm bar over cross-body" comes from the fact that in this technique your body is at a right angle to that of your opponent—in effect, creating a cross.

KARATE:
The "Power" Sport

A BRIEF HISTORY

DARUMA, AN INDIAN MONK, introduced the skills of a martial art to the monks of the Shao Lin monastery in China thousands of years ago. It was taught as a manner of developing strength and endurance. Daruma studied animal fighting positions and blended these with other combat techniques, teaching the Shao Lin monks so well that they became the most fearsome fighters in all of China.

A system of teaching was developed to keep the sport fairly secret and yet to allow it to be passed down to those whom the monks wished to know of it. The system was based on *kata*—set pieces and techniques of the martial art Daruma began. These *kata* could be practiced by the

KARATE: THE "POWER" SPORT

student without a partner. It was *kata* that enabled the techniques of Daruma to survive through the ages.

In the 1600's, the feudal lords on the island of Okinawa banned the use of all weapons. The martial art that Daruma developed spread to Okinawa and was called "Chinese hand," in tribute to the country where it first developed.

Modern karate was introduced to the Japanese public in 1922 by Master Funakoshi Gichin. He gave it the name *karate* (pronounced "kah-rah'-tay"), which means "open hand."

To Funakoshi, karate was not only a martial art, it was also a form of character development. He said:

> As a mirror's polished surface reflects whatever stands before it, and a quiet valley carries even small sounds, so must a student of karate render his mind empty of selfishness and wickedness in an effort to react appropriately towards anything he might encounter. This is the meaning of *kara* ("empty") in karate.

Funakoshi established his own school, which he called *Shotokan,* in Tokyo. *Shoto* was his nickname. *Kan* means "school." He died in 1957 at the age of eighty-eight, but *shotokan* karate survives. It is the most widely practiced and taught approach to karate in the West.

It was after World War II that karate spread to the United States and other countries throughout the world. Today there are a dozen or so main styles of karate.

KARATE: THE "POWER" SPORT

There is also the main contrast between self-defense karate and sport karate—basically the difference between street-fighting to defend yourself and competitive matches that are governed by strict rules. Most experts believe that all karate can be traced back to the time of the Shao Lin monastery and the teachings of the Indian monk Daruma.

THE NATURE OF THE SPORT

Since karate is so popular, finding and joining a karate club or school *(dojo)* should be quite easy for you. There, under the direction of a karate master *(sensei)*, you will get the proper guidance to learn the sport safely. The basic techniques of karate can be learned in a few months by any boy or girl, man or woman. Yet, you can spend a lifetime striving to perfect these techniques, which focus on punching *(tsuki)*, striking *(uchi)*, kicking *(keri)*, and blocking *(uke)*.

Karate is not a sport to show off with or to take lightly. It bears mentioning that so powerful are the hands of a karate expert that a blow delivered to the throat or head is capable of causing death or serious injury. Those skilled in karate can exert enough power to shatter boards and bricks with a single blow of the hand or foot.

Those persons really involved with karate realize that in addition to the sport being a magnificent form of self-defense, it is also an activity that strives for the harmonious development of body and mind. Both Zen and Yoga are many times joined with the practice of karate.

When Zen philosophy is applied to karate, you develop the ability to be calm under conditions of stress, while on the other hand, you are able to summon anger in a situation where anger is needed. This body-mind combination has been called "moving Zen."

Yoga also aids the body and mind in the effective practice of karate. As a beginner, you'll probably do a lot of complaining about the demands karate makes on your body and your mind. You'll have to develop the ability to raise your legs above the horizontal, to pivot your pelvis, to balance on one leg, to withstand a blow you know is coming. Yoga will help in all of these. Yoga will ease your tightened muscles, the strains and sprains, the bruised ego, the uncomfortable feelings.

THE KARATE SHOUT—THE KEE-UP (KIAI)

American Indians, Samurai warriors and other fighting peoples let loose shouts when running toward their enemies. This helped in the development of courage. Modern-day javelin throwers and weightlifters also use a form of this shout. *"Kiai"* is the karate form of this shout. A sudden expulsion of air from the lungs, the shout should come from the stomach and explode from

Karate Shout (Kiai): *tensed abdominal muscles in preparation for the thrust of exhaling.*

the mouth at the instant of attack or defense.

The *kiai* can frighten an opponent, can help your system get set, can help to reduce your fear, can assist in making you exert more force. But note: never say *"kee-up,"* which is like saying "shout."

You should practice and develop the *kiai* through breathing exercises several times a day. Raise your arms and tilt your head back. Inhale deeply through your nose or mouth. Lower your head. Press the held breath down by placing your hands on your stomach. The tension in the abdomen gives thrust when you exhale. There's always a bit more breath left. Exhale a final time to get it out. Practice this breathing exercise using good posture. Do it before training as well as several times daily.

THE UNIFORM AND THE BOW

Both the karate and judo uniforms are known as the *gi*. A double-breasted cotton jacket held together by a belt and a loose pair of cotton trousers form the white karate uniform. The pants are put on first and are tied at the front with the attached strings. The belt is tied with a square knot. You should always roll up the pants and jacket separately and tie them together with the belt in carrying the uniform from place to place. All beginners wear white belts. You then progress to yellow, green, purple, brown, and black. All the clothing you will need, except for the black belt, can be obtained from most sporting-goods stores.

Karate classes start and end with a bow. It is a sign of respect for the teacher, the other participants, the sport. The bow also indicates your sincerity toward the sport of karate.

THE STANCE (DACHI)

In football, basketball, baseball, ballet—the proper stance makes for the proper balance and the best results.

Stance in karate is especially important because of the kicks, the punches, the blocks. There are a number of stances; each one is designed for a different purpose. One main principle for stances is that you should keep your center of body-balance low—the area of your body just below the navel. This makes for ease of balance. Another general principle is that in all fighting stances, you should keep both hands at waist-level and at least one hand wrapped into a fist.

THE NATURAL OR EVERYDAY STANCE *(Hachiji-Dachi)*

The natural or everyday stance in karate resembles normal posture. Your feet are placed about a shoulder's width apart, toes turned slightly outward. Your fists are slightly in front of your body. From this position you will be able to move efficiently into an offensive or defensive position.

THE FORWARD STANCE *(Zenkutsu-Dachi)*

The forward stance involves placing about 60 percent of your body weight on your front leg. Your rear leg is positioned straight up and kept rigid. Your heels are flat on the ground. Get down as low as possible, whether your movement is forward or back. You can make this easier on your body by bending your knees.

To advance from the left forward stance, position your

KARATE: THE "POWER" SPORT

Natural or Everyday Stance (Hachiji-Dachi): *this ready stance positions one effectively for offensive or defensive movement.*

right foot next to your left. Both knees remain bent. Continue your forward movement as you skim the surface of the ground with your foot and keep your right knee bent at a thirty-degree angle. At the instant your right foot touches the ground, extend and straighten your left leg.

The forward stance is used for offense and defense. The length of stride (width between your two feet) in the forward stance is approximately the width of your shoulders. By reversing your moves, you can go backward from the forward stance.

Forward Stance (Zenkutsu-Dachi): *at the instant the right foot touches the ground, the left leg is extended and straightened.*

THE CAT STANCE *(Neko-Ashi-Dachi)*

The cat stance is mainly defensive. Move into this stance from the natural position by placing your left foot approximately six inches behind your right heel. Point your toes forward. Raise your right heel. You are thus in a front-facing position, with your left-foot toes pointed sideways. The final result of these maneuvers is that you face your opponent with rear knee bent, leg tense, body half-front.

Cat Stance (Neko-Ashi-Dachi): *three different views of this stance showcase defensive value and its feline qualities.*

Straddle-Leg Stance (Kiba-Dachi): *strength comes from the bow-like effect of anchored feet and knees bent outward.*

THE STRADDLE-LEG STANCE *(Kiba-Dachi)*

The straddle-leg stance is especially effective for sideward moves. Your legs are spread a distance equal to twice the width of your shoulders. Get your heels firmly on the ground. Point your toes straight ahead. Bend your knees out and balance your weight equally on both legs. Your leg and hip muscles should be tightened. Your back should be straight, and your chest should be thrust forward. It is important that your knees be positioned directly over your big toes. Strength in the stance comes from the bow-like effect of your anchored feet and your knees bending outward.

THE HOUR-GLASS STANCE *(Sanchin-Dachi)*

The hour-glass stance uses the reverse tension of the straddle-leg stance and provides thrust to the outside. You tense your knees inward, positioning your front knee directly over your toes and your rear knee two inches forward of your toes. Your body weight is distributed equally. Point your toes inward and get your front heel and rear toes almost even with each other. The heels should be positioned about shoulder-width apart.

Variations of the straddle-leg stance and the hour-glass stance are the wide hour-glass stance *(Hangetsu-Dachi)*, in which you spread your legs twice shoulder width, and the diagonal straddle-leg stance *(Sochin-Dachi)*, which has the look of the straddle-leg stance twisted forward. A major variation in the latter is that your rear knee is nearly twelve inches forward of your big toe, and your front knee is almost directly over your big toe.

THE HORSE STANCE *(Dachi)*

The horse stance gets its name from the appearance of this move, in which you are positioned as if you are riding a horse. Get your feet positioned almost two

Horse Stance (Kubu-Dachi): *stability of this stance comes from the low center of gravity and the wide but firmly flexed outward movement of the legs.*

shoulder-widths apart. Your back is straight; you are lowered in a squat; your toes point straight ahead. Firm your legs so that they flex outward and keep your feet steady. Get your knees to line up above your big toes.

Movement out of the horse stance starts with you turning your head to the vicinity in which you wish to move. If you wish to go left, for example, position your left leg across and in front of your right. Next, move your right leg to get back to your original position, still maintaining your feet spread about two shoulder-widths apart.

Back Stance (Kōkutsu-Dachi): *mo*
weight is placed on bent rear leg

THE BACK STANCE *(Kōkutsu-Dachi)*

The back stance is a basic position from which beginners can benefit greatly. It is a stance that will help you master many karate techniques. About 70 percent of your weight is placed on your bent rear leg. Your upper body should be straight and faced half-front. Your hips should be locked in a 45-degree angle. The toes of your front leg are positioned in a straight line with the heel of your rear foot. Don't allow the toes of the back foot to point toward the rear, or you will have problems in tensing that leg properly as you move back and forth.

As you move in this stance, move your hips first. Shift your entire body weight in the direction of the movement. Do not pick up your foot. Keep both knees bent. Glide and slide. Shift your weight to your front leg as your back leg comes forward.

Your fists are clenched and your arms are aligned with your thighs as you make your moves in the back stance. After many practices of this stance, you will become expert at it, and you will be able to tense and then relax your body with very little effort.

For a beginner in karate, it is best to work with one stance. Perfect that stance and then switch to another. This approach will prevent you from getting the different aspects of the different stances mixed up. The back stance is perhaps the best one to begin with. It gives you a good foundation from which to block punches and to launch punches and kicks. Ultimately, you should learn and perfect as many stances as possible for different competitions and situations.

THE KARATE FIST

The karate fist is essential for both offense and defense, and it is very important that you form it properly. Start with your hand in an open position, as if you were getting

Karate Fist: essential for both offense and defense.

ready to shake hands. Then roll your fingers into a ball. Press your thumb against the rolled-up index and middle fingers—and you have formed the karate fist.

There are a few precautions to keep in mind concerning the fist. Your wrist should be tightened and your fist should be firmly clenched to prevent hurting your fingers when you land a punch. Mainly use the first two knuckles when you strike a punch, and squeeze them as tight as possible so that they are almost flat and square.

It is possible to draw an imaginary straight line down the middle of your forearm to a midpoint between your forefinger and middle-finger knuckles. In striking out, a straight line is formed by your forearm and knuckles. Force and power come from the straightness of this line—you actually transmit the maximum strength of your body through your arm to the wrist and into the face of your forefist *(seiken).*

PUNCHING (ZUKI)

You may have seen demonstrations in which wood or bricks have been shattered into pieces by powerful punches. These demonstrations were done by masters. Don't ever attempt to smash wood or bricks—you won't break anything except your hand. As a beginner, you are not ready for the unloading of such devastating power.

Another punching rule you should follow as a beginner is that you should start by simulating your punch: that is, not actually landing it, but going through all the motions.

A third set of principles involves the practicing of punches. Avoid extending your arms when practicing any of the karate punches; too much stress and pressure is placed on the joints of your body. Get into the habit of holding back the striking arm in practice situations. Never unload with the full impact you are capable of. You should also stay away from practicing punches while you are moving until you have mastered the ability to punch effectively from a standing position.

Finally, remember that each punch you land should be delivered with maximum power and concentration. Karate philosophy states that one good shot is better than a bunch of sloppy, weak blows. A general operating rule for all punches is to harness power, concentration, and control into one big punch. The result will be devastating to your opponent.

THE STRAIGHT PUNCH *(Seiken-Choku-Zuki)*

Start out from the natural stance. Extend your left hand, palm-down, in front of your body. Put your cocked right fist just above your right hip.

Extend your right arm and start to deliver the punch in a straight line, with your palm up. Twist your right wrist as your elbow passes upward above your stomach. At this moment, you should pull your cocked left hand halfway back to your hip. Your fist should make contact with the palm facing downward. Your left hand should be pulled back in a readied and cocked posistion on your left hip.

Note that at the moment of contact, the tensed body muscles, the withdrawn arm, and the twisting blow's speed all combine to make for a fully concentrated, powerful punch. This maximum concentration of force is called the Point of Focus in karate. At the conclusion of your punch, relax all your muscles so that your body will be able to respond easily to the next move.

A straight punch with the left fist follows the same

procedure: left fist thrust forward, right fist pulled back to the right side.

THE STEPPING PUNCH *(Oi-Zuki)*

The stepping punch is often employed when you close in on an opponent. You keep both feet solidly on the ground, advancing your left foot and stretching out your left arm. Clench both fists. Begin the punch by moving your right leg and arm forward. Your right arm should brush lightly against your left leg. Your right fist should pass against your waist.

Focus the punch the instant your advancing foot touches the ground. The whole procedure requires that fast, free movement. Your back should be straight; you should not overreach. At the moment your punch makes contact, tighten all muscles and then relax them to be ready for the next move.

THE REVERSE PUNCH *(Gyaku-Zuki)*

Very much like the stepping punch, this is perhaps a *karateka*'s most potent weapon. It has counterattack value in that it can be delivered after you block an attack from an opponent. It is a punch that comes off the hand opposite to the leading foot.

Get into a low forward stance with your left arm extended. Pull back your right fist just above your hip, which should be held at a 45-degree angle. Shoot your

Reverse Punch (Gyaku-Zuki): *comes from hand opposite the leading foot.*

Gyaku-Zuki: *right fist is pulled back; the stance is low and forward.*

right fist out in a straight line and pull your left clenched hand back. Twist your right hip forward, arms close to the body, back straight, feet in the same position. As your right arm goes forward, you should twist your wrist and push back hard on your rear foot. At the moment of impact, your body should be facing directly forward.

Good technique for the reverse punch is a flowing motion and a relaxed body until the moment you throw the punch.

Hook Punch (Kagi-Zuki): *punching arm is tight against the body and back is straight.*

THE HOOK PUNCH *(Kagi-Zuki)*

Effective in close quarters, the hook punch is a variation of the straight punch. The key differences are that you hook your punching hand tightly to the inside as your elbow passes your stomach, and that your punching arm is tight against your body. Remember to hold your back straight in delivering this punch. The head, the neck, and the side of your opponent are prime target areas for the hook punch.

"U"-Punch (Yama-Zuki): *arms form the letter U.*

THE "U"-PUNCH *(Yama-Zuki)*

The name of this punch comes from the fact that your arms form the letter U as you punch. This punching technique gives you the opportunity to land two punches for the price of one: one blow from one fist can land on your opponent's face at the same time the other fist lands on your opponent's groin or stomach.

Operate out of the forward stance. Put both fists over your right hip. Pitch your body-weight forward. Extend your arms in a U shape. Double punch. Your right fist should go for the face. Your left fist should be face up and aimed at the stomach or groin.

STRIKING (UCHI)

The ability to strike effectively has been called the life-blood of karate. Without this ability, you have very little offense, and your opponent needs very little defense. Thus, strikes must be practiced and perfected.

BACK-FIST STRIKE *(Riken-Uchi)*

Useful against soft-target areas, the face and stomach in particular, the back-fist strike can dazzle an opponent with its surprise and speed. Position yourself with arms crossed over your chest. Your striking fist should be closed, with the palm facing backward and your first two knuckles ready as a striking surface.

Snap your elbow and start to move into the strike. At this time, your nonstriking hand should move into position near your hip. The whole technique is a speedy, half-circle blow, snapped out by the elbow and the forearm. Remember to keep a slightly bent elbow after you complete the strike to reduce elbow-joint strain.

BOTTOM-FIST STRIKE, OR FIST HAMMER *(Tettsui-Uchi)*

Begun from the same position and in the same manner as the back-fist strike, this maneuver enables you to strike sideways or straight down. The target areas are bony parts of the body—rib cage, shoulder blades—but you can get it off to the neck and face, too.

The bottom-fist strike is exactly what it sounds like—a strike with the bottom of the fist. The main difference from the back-fist strike is that you must twist-snap your wrist to get the bottom part of your fist to face up. Remember, tense your shoulder muscles and snap the blow in a half-circle movement.

KNIFEHAND STRIKE *(Shutō-Uchi)*

This is an effective openhanded technique for both offense and defense. To form the knifehand edge, do the following:

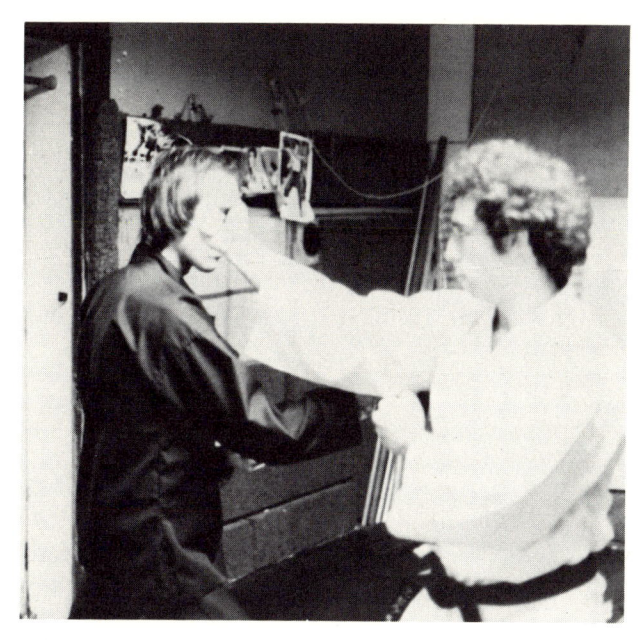

Bottom-Fist Strike, or Fist Hammer (Tettsui-Uchi): *although target areas are the rib cage and shoulder blades, this strike can be made at the neck and face, too.*

1. Open your palm.
2. Press your fingers tightly together.
3. Tuck your thumb down and press back.
4. Bend your first and second joint, never your third.
5. Keep your hand tightened to avoid injury. The striking areas are the back of the hand, the palm, the fingertips, and the hand's outer edge.

Your cocked right hand is positioned over your left shoulder, behind the ear. Your palm faces your cheek. Don't raise your shoulder, for this will prevent you from tensing your chest muscles during the strike. Rotate your stance slightly to the left. Swing your striking arm in a circular outside arc at the neck, head, or kidneys of your opponent. During the strike maneuver, turn your hand to get your palm up at the moment of impact. To avoid injury, be careful not to lock your elbow as you strike. In the knifehand strikes, force comes from the quick snap of elbow and wrist. It's similar to whiplashing with your arm.

THE PALM-HEEL STRIKE *(Teishō-Uchi)*

This is essentially a defensive maneuver that you should use with caution. The target area is an upward strike to the jaw or a side strike to the ribs. You use the heel of your palm as the striking surface.

Get into a natural stance. Your left palm should be placed in front of your body. Your right arm should be forward. Twist your wrist to point your fingers upward. Thrust out your right arm—palm heel straight out. In the same motion, snap back your left arm to position your fist on your hip.

ELBOW STRIKES *(Empi-Uchi)*

Easy to learn, elbow strikes are effective self-defense maneuvers used in close fighting. They can be directed to the front, side, or rear of an opponent and can be delivered in a forward, backward, up, down, or sideward position.

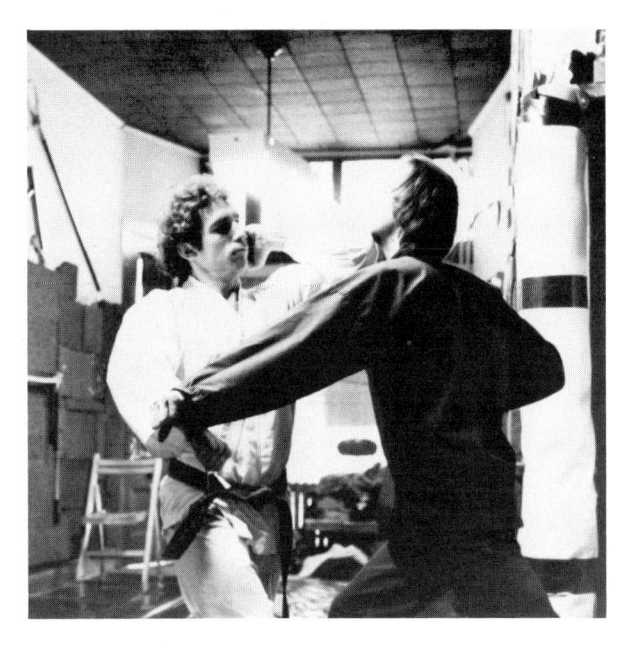

Elbow Strike (Empi-Uchi): *an upward strike aimed at the middle of the chin.*

Forward: The target area is generally the ribs or stomach. You swing out your relaxed arm and jam your elbow forward. Turn your wrist and tense your arm to get more force into the strike.

Backward: Delivered at the same target areas as the forward elbow strike, this maneuver begins by a quick lowering of your body. Keep your elbow close to your body and move it back in a straight line to the target area. Be ready to switch to the other elbow if your opponent has moved.

Downward: The point of your elbow is aimed at the

spine or neck of your opponent. Get into a forward stance and raise your fist straight over your head. Then push your elbow down toward your opponent. Note: don't keep your elbow alongside your body; keep it about six inches from your body.

Sideward: This maneuver comes off the natural stance. Cross your arms high in front of your body. Both elbows should point out. Keep your elbow in a straight line as you thrust sideways at your opponent. Note: as you attack, you should get into the horse stance for stronger side-balance.

Upward: This strike is aimed at the middle of the chin. Start with your fist at your hip and then zip your arm up. Turning your wrist to get your palm to line up with your ear, bend your elbow to get into a direct line with the target area. Make contact.

BLOCKING (UKE)

Using your hands and arms to block blows is the essence of blocking in karate. Since karate is a very effective self-defense sport, it employs several different types of blocks. A few key principles of blocking are:

1. Provide a smaller target by moving your body in a 45-degree angle.

2. The blocking hand should be on the same side as

your forward foot. Thus, left-foot-forward equals left-hand blocks, which makes for stronger balance and better blocking.

3. Relax your body, concentrating your power in the area where your blocking will take place.

4. Anticipate the move of your opponent. Be aware of where a blow is coming from so that you will be able to block it effectively.

5. Use a lot of force in your block to discourage your opponent. You can stop further attacks by "punishing"

ow Block (Gedan-Barai): *firmed arm muscles help focus the strength of the 'ock; it is effective against blows aimed at the lower part of the body.*

your opponent's arm or leg with a forceful block.

6. Realize the many different purposes of blocks and put all of these to use as the need arises. You can off-balance an opponent with a block. You can block and then stop an attack that is beginning. You can block and then retreat and set up for a counter-move. You can frustrate an opponent by using blocking to deflect his maximum force.

7. Practice blocking moves slowly at first and then increase your speed as you become more skilled. Each

Forearm Block (Ude-Uke): *inside edge of the forearm is the blocking area that provides protection for the chest and stomach.*

step in blocking should be made as rapidly as possible. However, when you are learning, correctness comes before speed.

THE LOW BLOCK *(Gedan-Barai)*

Effective against blows aimed at the lower part of your body, this movement starts from the natural stance. Position your right fist parallel to your left ear, palm facing the ear. Your other arm is extended straight out in front of you, the fist seven to eight inches from your thigh. Next, thrust your right blocking-arm down and across your chest, at the same time snapping back your left hand to your hip. The outer side of your fist and wrist, which are now about eight inches in front of your right thigh, becomes the blocking edge. Focus your strength here by firming your arm muscles.

FOREARM BLOCK (MIDDLE BLOCK) *(Ude-Uke)*

The inside edge of your forearm is your blocking area and offers chest and stomach protection. Assume the natural position. Raise your closed right fist up to your right ear, the knuckles out toward your opponent. Place your other arm straight out. Now sharply swing your right fist forward and slightly down. In the same motion, get more power by snapping back your left hand to your hip. Then twist your right forearm and blocking fist in a

KARATE: THE "POWER" SPORT

circle. Knuckles facing up, your fist should be approximately at shoulder level. At the point of contact, focus strongly.

HIGH BLOCK *(Age-Uke)*

Executed by most *karateka*s from the forward stance, the high block protects the face and neck. Cross your hands in front of your chest. Snap your blocking arm up, twisting your forearm inward. Switch your other hand to

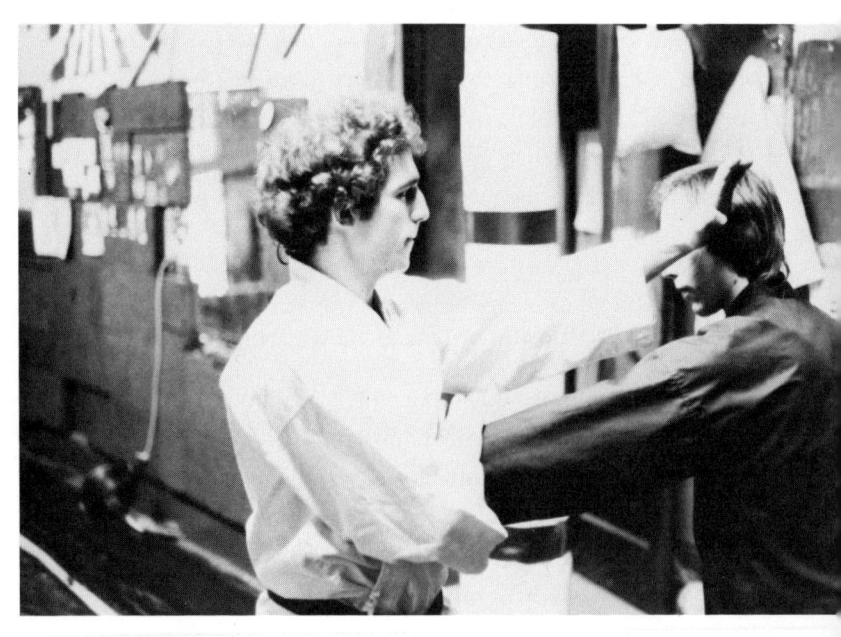

Knifehand Block (Shutō-Uke): *left arm moves down in an angle across che while right hand moves back to chest.*

your hip. The palm of your blocking hand should face your opponent and your block should focus with strength just above your head.

KNIFEHAND BLOCK *(Shutō-Uke)*

The knifehand block is most often used from a back stance or cat stance. You start by extending your right arm out in front of your body. Place your blocking left arm across your chest, the palm facing your right ear. Next, move your left knifehand down in an angle across your chest. Your elbow is the pivot—you twist and tense your forearm as the blow is delivered. Chest muscles are tense, the wrist is taut and straight. At the same time, move your right hand back to your chest with the palm up.

"X"-BLOCK *(Juji-Uke)*

Not much power is required for this effective and quick block against face- and neck-area attacks. A good advantage of the "X"-block is that you complete it with open hands, which places you in a good counterattacking position.

Begin the "X"-block from the ready stance by crossing your open hands in front of your chest. Next, shoot your hands up and keep the cross above your forehead. Your elbows should line up with your body. In this posi-

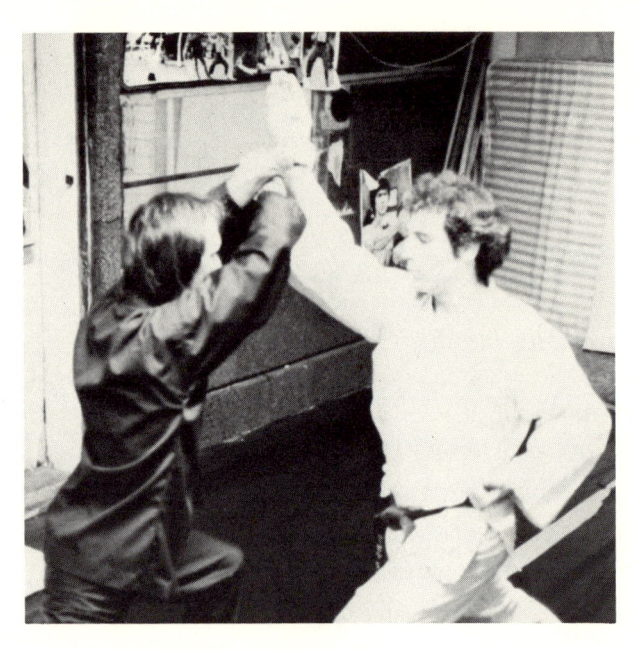

"X"-Block (Juji-Uke): *face and neck are securely protected by the X formed by hands positioned above forehead.*

tion, your face and neck are securely protected. Weak blocks result from elbows that are allowed to spread out too much.

Leg-Blocking Techniques

A special feature of karate is that offensive techniques can also be used as defensive techniques. Thus, while your feet can be used for attack, they can also be used to block and discourage attacks. Leg blocking is used many times when your hands can't do the job.

INSIDE SNAPPING BLOCK *(Nami Ashi)*

Speed and the fact that only the blocking leg is moved are two advantages of this maneuver. It is a good defensive move against a groin attack or a stamping attack. You use your knee as a spring and snap the bottom of your foot up in front of you. Return it quickly to its original position to be set for your next move. The inside snapping block can be used from several different free-style stances. In all of these stances, you do not have to shift any body weight.

CRESCENT-KICK BLOCK *(Mikazuki Geri Uke)*

The most popular of all foot-blocking moves is the crescent kick. You use the sole of your foot as the blocking surface. Basic blocking comes from the circular arc in which you swing your leg to ward off blows. Always remember to pull back your leg quickly after blocking with it.

A special feature of leg-blocking techniques is that they can easily be combined with offensive moves. Thus, a crescent kick and a side-thrust kick, for example, can be launched with the same leg.

Poised for kicking.

KICKING (GERI)

Kicking is one of the main areas that separates karate from other martial arts. Potent power comes from a karate master's feet—more power from the feet than from punches, as a general rule. More target areas also can be quickly reached. Always perform limbering-up kicking exercises before practicing kicking. Kick with caution. Remember the importance of the nonkicking leg as a

Front Kick (Mae-Geri): *striking surface is the ball of the foot...*

means of balance, and as a cushion for the impact shock of the kicking leg.

FRONT KICK *(Mae-Geri)*

Your striking surface is the ball of your foot. Target areas usually include chin, knee, groin, and solar plexus. Get into the natural position. Clench your fists. Raise your right (or kicking) knee as far as you can. Now snap your foot out—ankle flexed forward, body thrust out, back straight. At impact, tense your leg. After the kick, pull your foot back quickly to prevent it from being grabbed by your opponent. You can prevent injuries to your toes by keeping them curled upward.

The front kick can be performed either by snapping your knee up and thrusting forward or just by lashing your leg out without the snap. Both versions of the front kick enable you to strike with speed at a variety of target areas.

SIDE KICK *(Yoko-Geri)*

Like the front kick, you can execute the side kick with a snap or thrust motion. Target areas usually include face, ribs, knee, and solar plexus.

Standing sideways to your opponent, raise your right leg to about the knee-level of your stationary leg. Kick at your target in a straight line. Your striking surface will be the outer edge of your foot, so remember to pitch the flex of your ankle toward the inside of your leg. A split second before your knee straightens, pull back a bit on your leg to avoid injury to your knee ball-joint. Be aware that your leg should return to its raised position before you return it to the ground. Maintain careful balance and keep your eye on your opponent throughout the side-kick process.

ROUNDHOUSE KICK *(Mawashi-Geri)*

Key elements in this kick, which can be performed

Side Kick (Yoko-Geri): *force and power result from this kick.*

Roundhouse Kick (Mawashi-Geri): *hips swing, knee snaps; force and focus c into play as kick develops.*

with either foot, are the swinging of your hips and the snapping of your knees. You strike with the ball of your foot. Target areas include face, stomach, neck, and ribs.

Get into the natural or right-forward stance. Raise your bent leg, positioning your right arm toward the rear. Pivot your body forward. Swing halfway around on the ball of your left foot. Kick with a swinging motion of the hips and a snap of the knee. Bring the kicking leg back to the starting position before allowing it to touch the ground. This will aid your balance.

Back Kick (Ushiro-Geri): *target is concentrated on by player looking over his kicking-side shoulder.*

BACK KICK *(Ushiro-Geri)*

Employed most often against an attack from the rear, back-kick target areas include groin, chest, and stomach. You strike with your heel.

From the natural stance, bring your kicking foot to knee-level of the slightly bent supporting leg. Concentrate on your target by looking over your kicking-side shoulder. Now, in a straight line, thrust your kick out at your opponent. You should position your kicking leg at knee-level before allowing it to touch the ground.

STAMPING HEEL *(Fumikomi)*

The aim of this kick is to defend against grabbing attacks from the rear. Begin it from the natural stance. Bring your kicking foot to knee-level, keeping your eye on your target—your opponent's instep or shin. Plunge your heel down. In delivering this kick to the shin, strike with the inside edge of your foot as well as with your heel. A good way to master speed and control of the stamping-heel kick is to practice stopping your stamp just before your heel hits the floor or the target.

FLYING FRONT OR JUMP KICK *(Mae-Tobi-Geri)*

Executed with either foot, and invaluable as a surprise move, the flying front is initiated from the natural position. Bring one leg up so that its heel is at knee-level of the supporting leg. Leap into the air. Push hard with the supporting leg, which, when it reaches midair, becomes the leg that does the kicking. Move back the kicking leg so that you will be able to land on the ground with both feet in a balanced position.

Finally, these *key principles of kicking techniques* are worth stressing:

Stamping Heel (Fumikomi): *developing and end-point—effective self-defense against attacks from the rear.*

1. Keep your supporting leg slightly bent and firmly anchored to the ground.

2. Focus your eyes on your target before you start your kick in order to deliver an accurate blow.

3. Be aware of the need and importance of body balance throughout the kicking technique.

4. Get your hips into the kick for greatest power.

SPARRING (KUMITE)

After advancing in your karate training, you will be ready to develop the skills of sparring. The ability to anticipate the moves of an opponent and concentration and discipline are needed for you to be able to spar.

There are three types of sparring: Basic Sparring *(Kihon-Kumite),* Semifree Sparring *(Jiyū-Ippon Kumite),* and Freestyle Sparring *(Jiyu-Kumite).* In each of these, you will learn to attack and fend off attacks made against you. Sparring should not be engaged in until you have mastered the basics of blocking and attacking skills.

Basic sparring (and often semifree sparring) involves facing an opponent at a set distance and switching roles in attacking and defending on the basis of previously agreed-upon techniques. Freestyle sparring is different. There are no previously agreed-upon moves. You will attempt to score a "killing blow" on your opponent. However, in freestyle, as in the other forms of sparring, all blows must be stopped just before the point of contact, to avoid injuring your opponent. A person really skilled in karate has this ability to stop a blow the instant before it lands on his target.

Freestyle sparring is the most exciting and the most demanding of karate techniques, in the opinion of many. You put all your skills together and practice techniques with speed and power without causing any damage to your opponent. It is recommended that all free-sparring be engaged in under the supervision of a karate master.

THE ENERGY OF KARATE

Throughout the performance of karate skills—punches, kicks, strikes, blocks—key principles wedding your body and mind together are in operation. You should learn, understand, and put into practice these principles.

RHYTHM

Strength must always be applied at the most appropriate moment. Move gracefully from technique to technique. Control your body speed according to the ebb and flow of your actions. In baseball, for example, experts talk about a pitcher having good rhythm, of being in the groove, of just laying back and rocking pitches in effortlessly. This same rhythm operates as part of the energy of karate.

KARATE: THE "POWER" SPORT

TIMING

You must time your moves, and the placement of your body, with care. In baseball, a batter swinging a fraction of a second too soon or too late might find the result to be the difference between a home run and a foul ball. In karate, an error in timing can spell disaster. Timing is thus an important part of the energy of karate.

TANDEM HITTING

The expression "get your hips into it" is a simple way of explaining the force of tandem hitting. Your body's center of gravity is the area behind your navel. Performing karate moves, you summon tandem-hitting energy through an interlocking of pelvic and hip bones supported by your thigh, with your spine supporting your trunk. This correct "posture" produces maximum power. This is another part of karate energy.

SPEED AND POWER

In general, the more speed you can summon, the more power you can deliver. The longer the distance a blow travels to its target, the more speed can be generated. An arm or leg that is fully stretched delivers more of a blow than an arm or leg that is partially uncocked. You should practice quick, short thrusts at the punching board to develop speed and power. In baseball, some batters show off in batting practice and hit sky-high fly balls. Others whip their bats around, driving the ball with power to produce line drives. You can be a "high fly ball" karate hitter or you can harness speed and power and produce another important part of the energy of karate.

FOCUS POWER

Total body strength should be focused in delivering a blow. Baseball once again offers a good comparison. Some batters swing at a ball using only their arms to

ath, mind, and body focus—all combine in karate.

produce power; they are called "Punch-and-Judy" hitters. Other players get their whole body into their swing—Hank Aaron was a good example. His hips, wrists, buttocks—all of him went around into a flowing and powerful swing.

In karate, the use of just the arm for a punch or just the leg for a kick makes for a weak blow. Get all you have into it. Loose muscles are also important—they should be released and relaxed at the time of contact to prime your body to react again.

All of these factors make for energy. The more energy, the better and more effective the karate performance.

PSYCHOLOGICAL ENERGY OF KARATE

Karate trains the body. Karate also trains the mind. All things being equal physically, a person trained to harness the psychological energy of karate will find it a tremendous source of power. Three basic concepts operate as part of this psychological energy.

A MIND LIKE WATER *(Mizu No Kokoro)*

Ancient teachers of karate stressed the need to have a calm and undisturbed mind, like the surface of peaceful and reflecting water. Smooth, still water is like a mirror that shows clearly everything around it. If your mind is kept in this condition, you will be able to see and sense the physical and psychological movements and conditions of your opponent. This is part of your psychological energy.

A MIND LIKE THE MOON *(Tsuki No Kokoro)*

This concept is a clue to the way you can raise your consciousness. Moonlight reflects clearly on all things around it. Its beams make for clarity. A mental attitude that is "moonlike" makes you aware of how your opponent operates and clearly reveals defensive openings.

MIND AND WILL AS A UNIFIED FORCE

Two-way communication between the mind and the will must always be in operation. The mind understands, but without the will in force there is a short-circuit in the transmission of psychological energy.

Understand these concepts of basic psychological energy and put them into practice. Your karate performance will be better for it.

Tips from the Pros

THIS SECTION is a collection of advice, explanations, qualifications, theories, and "bread-and-butter" hints obtained form scores of interviews with judo and karate masters. Some of these tips are fundamental; others provide the logic and the common sense behind the mystique that some feel surrounds the martial arts.

1. Pushing and pulling at the proper time in judo can effectively put "application of maximum efficiency with a minimum of effort" into practice as an operating factor for you. You should push if your opponent pulls. You should pull if your opponent pushes. Add your force to that of your opponent. If you push at your opponent, allow him or her to push back. Then, as he or she pushes back, add your pulling to this pushing. You might wish to try on a friend the following specific example: Make a

loop with the thumb and middle finger of either hand. Invite your friend to attempt to pull your fingers apart. If your friend pulls, go in the direction of his pulling. Your friend will find it almost impossible to break your loop.

2. Karate theory states that the body's greatest strength can be concentrated in the area of a vertical line drawn directly down the front and center of the body. Your blows should, if at all possible, aim at this target area and follow this principle.

3. Physics operates in karate punching both in theory and in practice. When you withdraw one hand while punching with the other, the applicable physics theory is that for every action there is an equal and opposite reaction. Strive for as much force as possible in the hand that is pulled back. This will make for more strength in the punching hand.

4. Karate calls for a lot of shifting of body weight. Balance, smooth movements, keeping your hips in a straight line and holding correct posture—all of these should become part of your method of operation in the shifting of body weight.

5. Application of a karate technique that does not utilize all your energy concentrated at the same time *(Kime)* is so much wasted effort. Breath, mind, and body focus should all go into your movements.

6. Throwing techniques can work to your advantage in karate. Follow this sequence: Launch an attack; react to the block of your opponent by throwing him; focus all your power in a counterattack.

7. A famous karate expression states: "Move the hips first and the hands and feet last." This should always be put into practice for maximum concentration of strength. Hand and foot muscles are quick, but they are not as powerful as those in your pelvic and abdominal region. However, if you move the hips first and thus activate their power, you can then transfer this power to the faster but weaker muscles in your hands and feet.

8. Hitting with an open hand is vastly superior to hitting with a clenched fist. You can get more force into your blow and avoid hurting yourself by hitting with the open hand instead of the closed fist. More body areas can be reached with the open hand. If you are forced into a street fight, greater safety against injury also operates for you.

9. Always twist your forearm inward the instant before completing a punch. This snap-twist is an asset to the speed of the punch. Punching force is more stable and more forceful because you are twisting and thrusting out with your arm at about the same moment. This technique also makes it easier for you to tense arm and chest muscles at the moment of contact.

10. Reverse-punch technique can be improved if you practice your timing. It is important that you coordinate the forward twisting of your hips with your punching.

11. Know and observe the differences between striking and punching in karate. Punching sends force in a straight line through the forearm to the target area. Strik-

ing sends force laterally; generally, a snapping motion of the elbow is used in this technique.

12. The knifehand block is a classic example of the flow of karate—defense-offense in execution. Step back from a punching attack; block with the knifehand and then go into your counterattack from the back stance, using your front leg.

13. In all karate kicks, always get your kicking-leg's knee to your chest before lowering the leg to the ground. This will help prevent your opponent from grabbing your leg. It will also aid your balance.

14. Many Oriental martial arts are in some way related to karate through similarities in style and technique. A plus in learning karate is that you can move more easily from that skill into another martial art. It is best to learn one art first and then move on to another to avoid confusion and distraction.

15. Judo is a very fine complement to karate. Both sports are skills in their own right, but judo techniques applied to karate skills form a potent partnership.

16. Abdominal breathing is not just something to put into play when you are involved with judo or karate. It is a technique for better health and body development. Practice abdominal breathing in various life situations. When you walk down the street—walk, in effect, from the power of your abdomen, not just from the muscles in your legs. Just look at the way your stomach rises and falls as you breathe naturally and normally. What hap-

pens is that air presses the upper lungs and moves into the abdominal region. With practice, you can develop abdominal breathing in different life situations—walking, waiting for a bus, talking to a friend. Work on getting a greater amount of air into your lower lungs.

17. It is not a sign of conceit to spend some of your time looking at yourself in a full-length mirror. Analysis of your moves and your form will be much easier if you can see how you look in the looking-glass.

18. Beware of martial-arts schools that offer little choice in programs or have few students in attendance. You should not sign up at a *dojo* where there is just one three-year program, for example. Ask about options. Determine if there are make-up lessons. Be wary about time limits. Realize that in karate, for example, you are better off with quite a few partners to train with. If the class is so small that you can count the number of students on one hand, that is not the school for you.

19. Balance is vitally affected by the way you position your legs in the various karate stances. If your legs are too far apart, your muscles cannot be tensed correctly; quick movement is reduced and the stance is weakened. On the other hand, if you get your legs too close together, balance is not stable because the body's center of gravity is too high.

Glossary

JUDO

ASHIWAZA—foot-throw techniques
DAN—degree
DOJO—practice or exercise hall
GATAME—mat-work holding technique
GI—the judo uniform
IPPON—one full point in a competitive match
JIGO TAI—defensive stance or posture
JUDOKA—one who practices judo
KAESHIWAZA—techniques for counterattack
KAKE—technique application
KAPPO—a system of artificial respiration
KATA—training techniques of formal, prearranged movements

GLOSSARY

KODOKAN—administration center of world judo, located in Tokyo
KOSHIWAZA—hip-throw techniques
KUZUSHI—moment of completely breaking an opponent's balance
KWANSETUWAZA—the art of locking an opponent
KYU—a degree for a pupil
MATTAI—sign of submission, literally "enough" or "I surrender."
MUNDANSHA—a *judoka* below black-belt rank
NAGE WAZA—throwing techniques
NEWAZA—groundwork
NIPPON DEN KODOKAN JUDO—the formal and full name for recognized world judo
OSAE KOMI WAZA—hold-down techniques
RANDORI—free play, fighting practice
REI—bow
SAMURAI—Japanese feudal warrior
SENSEI—teacher or instructor
SHIAI—a contest or competitive match
SHIHAN—master
SHIMEWAZA—strangulation or choking techniques
SHINTAI—advancing and retreating
SURI ASHI—sliding foot movements
SUTEMIWAZA—sacrifice throws
TACHI REI—bow from standing position
TACHIWAZA—techniques of throwing
TATAMI—straw mat for practicing judo
TORI—one who applies judo techniques; the thrower

TSUKURI—the technique of breaking an opponent's balance
UKE—the person to whom techniques are applied; the one thrown
UKEMI—breakfalls; the art of falling
WAZA—techniques
WAZA ARI—the half-point in competition
WAZARI AWASETE IPPON—two half-points that equal an *ippon* (one full point) and determine a contest winner
YUDANSHA—a person who holds a black-belt degree
ZA-REI—a bow from the sitting position

KARATE

BUDO—"way of the warrior"
CHOSHI—rhythm
DO—"the way"
DOJO—karate school
FUDO-DACHI—an immovable stance
GI—karate uniform
HACHIJI-DACHI—natural stance
HYOSHI—timing
JIYU KUMITE—free-sparring
JUTSU—technique
KAMAE—fixed posture or stance
KATA—set pieces and techniques, form
KEIKO—practice

GLOSSARY

KEIREI—bow
KERI—striking
KI—vital energy
KIME—point of focus, maximum concentration of force
KUMITE—sparring
NAGEWAZA—techniques of throwing
REI—ceremonial bow
REIGI—politeness, courtesy
RENSHU—training
SENSEI—teacher
SUKI—opening
TSUKI—punching
UCHI—striking
UKE—blocking
YOI—ready posture

Appendix A

SUMMARY SKETCHES OF FOUR OTHER EASTERN MARTIAL ARTS

KUNG FU Chinese. *Kung* ("master"), *fu* ("man")—literally means "master of man" or "master of self." Open fist. Half-moves designed for use with weapons such as spears, swords. Little free-fighting. Intended after years of fighting to create internal power. Smooth and slow movements.

TAE KWAN DO Korean. *Tae* ("book"), *kwan* ("fist"), *do* ("martial art"). Many combined moves prearranged, then applied to free-fighting. Sharp movements. Evolved over a thousand years ago from Korean foot-fighting.

APPENDIX A

                Special focus on foot techniques such as hook kick.

KENDO   Japanese. "Way of the sword." Uses samurai warrior techniques: hair-trigger coordination, disciplined mind, whiplike attacks and parries. Combatants today use bamboo sword, heavy cloth, and bamboo armor. Sport seeks to give complete physical and mental control to practitioners.

AIKIDO   Japanese. Originated in 1883 as a form of physical defense and exercise and also as a deeply spiritual action. *Ai* ("harmony"), *ki* ("spirit"), *do* ("way")—"way of martial spiritual harmony." Aikido expert turns attacker's power against the attacker, taking away weapons.

Appendix B

JUDO CONTEST CALLS

FUSEN-SHO—win by default
HAJIME—start
HANTEI—decision or judgment
HIKIWAKE—draw
IPPON—one point
JIKAN—time
KOKA—one-eighth point
MATE—wait
OSAEKOMI—holding
OSAEKOMI-TOKETA—loosened, lost, ineffective hold
SONO-MAMA—do not move, stop
SORE-MADE—stop, that's it!
WAZA ARI—one-half point
YOSHI—continue, go ahead, all right
YUKU—one-quarter point
YUSEI-GACHI—win by superiority

HARVEY FROMMER

A veteran of 1,001 street fights as a kid growing up in Brooklyn, Harvey Frommer is a professor at the City University of New York, holding a Ph.D. in media and communications. A former United Press sportswriter, Dr. Frommer's articles and stories have appeared in newspapers all over America. His book credits include *A Baseball Century: the First Hundred Years of the National League* and *A Sailing Primer*. He is currently at work on a dictionary of sports language and a book on soccer.